WITHDRAWN

The Letters of
John Hamilton Reynolds

The Letters of
John Hamilton Reynolds

Edited with an introduction by

Leonidas M. Jones

UNIVERSITY OF NEBRASKA PRESS · LINCOLN

Contents

Abbreviations and Common Shortened References

AL: autograph letter.

ALS: autograph letter, signed.

Champneys: Basil Champneys, *The Memoirs and Correspondence of Coventry Patmore*, 2 vols. (London: Bell, 1900).

Forman, *Letters of Keats*: Maurice Buxton Forman, ed., *The Letters of John Keats*, 4th ed. (London: Oxford University Press, 1952).

Gittings: Robert Gittings, "The Poetry of John Hamilton Reynolds," *Ariel*, I (1970), 7–17. This new journal is published at the University of Bristol.

Hudnall: Clayton E. Hudnall, "John Hamilton Reynolds, James Rice, and Benjamin Bailey in the Leigh Browne–Lockyer Collection," *Keats-Shelley Journal*, XIX (1970), 11–39.

KC: Hyder E. Rollins, ed., *The Keats Circle*, 2d ed., 2 vols. (Cambridge, Mass.: Harvard University Press, 1965).

Letters: Hyder E. Rollins, ed., *The Letters of John Keats*, 2 vols. (Cambridge, Mass.: Harvard University Press, 1958).

Marsh, *J. H. R.*: *Poetry and Prose*: George L. Marsh, *John Hamilton Reynolds: Poetry and Prose* (London: Oxford University Press, 1928).

Selected Prose: Leonidas M. Jones, ed., *Selected Prose of John Hamilton Reynolds* (Cambridge, Mass.: Harvard University Press, 1966).

Shelley: Henry C. Shelley, *Literary By-paths in Old England* (Boston: Little, Brown, and Co., 1906).

Introduction

John Hamilton Reynolds and the Keats Circle

John Hamilton Reynolds's father's family background entitled him to his place as a member of the Cockney school of English poetry. His great-grandfather, Thomas Reynolds, was a tanner of Tottenham, and his grandfather, Noble Reynolds, a barber of the same parish.[1] His father, George, after attending Christ's Hospital from 1774 to 1779, taught school for most of his long life in London at the Lambeth Boys Parochial School, the Lambeth Female Asylum, and at Christ's Hospital, though from the early 1790s until about 1806 he left the city to teach at Shrewsbury School. Active in his profession, he was a specialist in the Bell system of education, who was once sent by Christ's Hospital to introduce the plan at Hertford School, and he published six school books,[2] one of which the *Edinburgh Review* listed in the same announcement of new books as Keats's *Endymion*.[3] In his family life, however, he was quiet and unassertive; Keats does not mention him even once during all the time he visited in his houses. His son delicately refrained from informing him when he interceded to try to prevent a reduction of his salary in 1820.[4] His "rooted objection to having his personal appearance delineated in any way" frustrated all Thomas Hood's attempts to have him sit for a portrait.[5]

Clearly the stronger spouse throughout their long life together was Charlotte Cox Reynolds, whom he married on

1. Guildhall Library, London, MS 5266, vol. 4; MS 5265, vol. 5; MS 5257, vol. 10; and MS 5257, vol. 11, as recorded in Robert Gittings, "The Poetry of John Hamilton Reynolds," *Ariel*, I (1970), 8–9 (hereafter cited as Gittings).

2. George L. Marsh, *John Hamilton Reynolds: Poetry and Prose* (London: Oxford University Press, 1928), pp. 10–11 (hereafter cited as *J. H. R.: Poetry and Prose*).

3. *Edinburgh Review*, XXX (June 1817), 260.

4. See p. 17 below.

5. Henry C. Shelley, *Literary By-paths in Old England* (Boston: Little, Brown, and Co., 1906), pp. 222–23 (hereafter cited as Shelley).

7 January 1790.[6] Four years older than her husband when she married at what was then the rather late age of twenty nine, she came from a family with pretensions superior to those of his humble origin. She was related by marriage to a distinguished Hamilton family whose descendents included the famous William Beckford and the sprightly writer on hunting, Peter Beckford, and she showed her pride in her connections in the middle names of two of her children, John Hamilton and Eliza Beckford Reynolds. Her only brother, William Beckford Cox, who established himself financially during military service in India and the East Indies, was the father of the sophisticated "Charmian" of Keats's letters.[7] While her husband remains almost unobserved in the wings, Mrs. Reynolds's more forceful personality figures prominently on stage in the records of Keats and Hood. And yet one ought to guard against exaggeration of her strong will which might result from Keats's reaction against her or from Hood's bitter quarrel with her in 1835. John F. M. Dovaston's "Lines to Mrs. Reynolds of Lambeth with a Goose" testifies to the happy home which she maintained for her husband as well as her children.[8] The character of Mrs. Morton in Reynolds's Edward Herbert essays, with her subordination of herself to her beloved husband despite her superior intellect, hints that Charlotte Reynolds was wise enough to treat her husband's ego carefully.[9] And Hood's early letters reveal that she was as loving and lovable as she was firm in the control of her household.

The single known record of George Reynolds in the years immediately following his graduation from Christ's Hospital in 1779 shows only that on 5 February 1788 he lived at Kingsland in the area of Hackney and Tottenham;[10] probably by that time he had already begun his long career of teaching in London schools which have not been identified. He was still in London on 28 November 1791, because the baptism of his first child, Jane, is recorded on that date.[11] Thereafter he moved the family to

6. Phyllis G. Mann, "The Reynolds Family," *Keats-Shelley Journal*, V (1956), 6.

7. Gittings, pp. 9–10.

8. John F. M. Dovaston, *Fitz-Gwarine, with Other Rhymes* (Shrewsbury, 1813).

9. Leonidas M. Jones, ed., *Selected Prose of John Hamilton Reynolds* (Cambridge, Mass.: Harvard University Press, 1966), pp. 309–11 (hereafter cited as *Selected Prose*).

10. Guildhall Library, MS 5265.

11. Mann, "The Reynolds Family," p. 7. Many records erroneously report the date of her birth as 1792.

Shrewsbury, where he taught in the school and where his first and only son, John Hamilton Reynolds, was born on 9 September 1794. Three other daughters were later born at Shrewsbury: Mariane[12] on 23 February 1797, Eliza Beckford in 1799, and Charlotte in 1802.

From his ninth through his twelfth years (1803–1806), John Hamilton Reynolds attended the Shrewsbury School, where his father taught. Two poems in the *London Magazine*, signed with Reynolds's pseudonym Ned Ward, Jr., cast some light on what life was like there for the young students.[13] In May 1823 Reynolds wrote "A Parthian Peep at Life, an Epistle to R——d A——n,"[14] recalling joyously their shared schoolboy activities, but by the next year the friend had died and in "Stanzas to the Memory of Richard Allen,"[15] he lamented the schoolmate who had been buried in a "country church-yard" under trees beneath which he had played as a boy. Although no Shrewsbury School record has been accessible to check on Richard Allen's attendance, it seems safe to conclude that in general Reynolds drew on his own experience at school, though nostalgia and poetic license may have colored some details. The activities recounted are by no means surprising—indeed, they are what one would expect of the usual schoolboys—but they are particular enough to deserve being specified. In "A Parthian Peep," he recalls playing on the walls, shooting marbles on the playground under the trees, reading romances in the shade, playing at the river's edge (the Severn), looking for birds' nests, stealing crab apples, and attending a school party with country dancing. Repeating some of the items like the marbles and searching for linnets in "Stanzas to the Memory of Richard Allen," he adds recollections of "wild Thursday afternoon" (evidently a half holiday), hunting, fishing, swimming, playing ball and prisoner's base, rolling hoops, climbing trees, and stealing apricots for a "pillow treat."

The poem "Old Ballads" included in a *London* essay[16] probably refers to Shrewsbury School too, though the experience may have occurred during his later attendance at St. Paul's. After

12. I follow Hyder Rollins in spelling the name as her son always spelled it. Keats and others spell it variously and inconsistently.

13. Leonidas M. Jones, "New Letters, Articles, and Poems by John Hamilton Reynolds," *Keats-Shelley Journal*, VI (1957), 103.

14. *London Magazine*, VII (May 1823), 525–26.

15. Ibid., IX (January 1824), 35–36.

16. Ibid., IV (July 1821), 8–9.

reading the ballads "under the play-ground tree," he would tell the stories to the other boys, undoubtedly interesting them the more because he was breaking the rule as he related the tales of *Chevy Chase* and Richard Plantagenet. The picture which emerges from the poems is one of a normal and happy school life.

The fullest account of life at Shrewsbury School at this time appears in *The Fancy* (1820), but one must be warier in dealing with the experiences of Peter Corcoran described there than was John Masefield, who accepted them all as Reynolds's own.[17] Although Peter Corcoran echoes Reynolds's life in many ways— both were born in September 1794, both were sent to Shrewsbury School, both had an avid interest in sports, and both were aspiring poets—the book is mock autobiography. Its theme, treated both comically and sentimentally, is the moral decay of Peter Corcoran, ending in rejection by his beloved and his death because of his increasing addiction to sports, especially the un-savory boxing. Anticipation of that theme undoubtedly led Reynolds to exaggerate some of his own misconduct and to add offenses of which he was innocent: young Peter tore grammars, broke bounds, pilfered orchards, fought, and swore. As the traditional servant to an older boy, he cleaned shoes, set the tea utensils, and prepared special treats for his supper. Also for his boy-master, he would slip out of the bedroom window at night to steal fruit for his tart, and he would carry the older boy's fighting cocks in a bag to a nearby field. Like Huck Finn and Tom Sawyer, he was very active at night, stealing out by moonlight to fish for trout and swim in the Severn. Because he did not study indus-triously, the headmaster punished him frequently with the rod, but his tutor, the Reverend Mr. S——, who was third master, was both kind and assiduous in counseling him and caring for him.[18] Although we cannot know which experiences were Reynolds's own, a summary of these activities in a biographical sketch is valuable because, after discounting the degree of mis-conduct, we are left with a sense of what life was like at Shrewsbury School when Reynolds attended.

Three other features of Peter's development at Shrewsbury are especially important because the appearance of the same traits in the later Reynolds argue that they were indeed based on personal schoolboy experience: the writing of verse, the desire for fame,

17. John Masefield, ed., *The Fancy* (London: Elkin Mathews, 1905).
18. *Selected Prose*, pp. 261–63.

and the sharp wit. Peter began writing verse at this early period: he lampooned his boyish enemies and he penned melancholy and heroic songs. Deeply gratified by the applause these efforts won from his schoolfellows, he was stirred early by a craving for fame. In like manner, his fighting with schoolmates was for glory, as well as for love of battle. His wit also began to win notice; no one could surpass him in smart remarks to the master's daughter or the maid.

It is certain that by 1809 the Reynolds family had returned from Shrewsbury to London because the Christ's Hospital record for that year includes a payment to George Reynolds of "£20 for visiting the Hertford school and introducing there Dr. Bell's system of education."[19] But probably the family had made the move earlier, in 1806 when John Hamilton finished at Shrewsbury School and enrolled at St. Paul's, where he remained until 1810. Later in life Richard Harris Barham, author of *The Ingoldsby Legends*, reported that Reynolds had been "an old schoolfellow of mine at St. Paul's School,"[20] but Barham probably did not know Reynolds at the school well, if at all, since he was six years Reynolds's senior and he left the school the year after Reynolds's arrival to enter Oxford in 1807. Richard Bentley, the same age as Reynolds, was evidently more nearly contemporary at St. Paul's, but the strictly businesslike tone of Reynolds's later letters to him in this volume argues that at most their acquaintance in school could have been slight.

Graduating from St. Paul's in 1810, Reynolds secured a junior clerkship in the Amicable Society for a Perpetual Assurance office not later than 18 July, the date on which he signed his first document. He continued to perform this clerical work until about 24 April 1816, the date of his last signature in the record.[21] The office was small as compared with Lamb's great East India House with its numerous clerks and huge tomes of accounts; the Amicable Society usually employed only three clerks at a time, among whom were John Griffin in 1810 and W. B. Wedlake in 1816. Reynolds evidently performed this mundane work capably from his sixteenth through his twenty-second year, if the fact that he signed most of the documents from 1810 through 1816 can be taken as evidence of his competence.

19. Marsh, *J. H. R.: Poetry and Prose*, p. 11.
20. Richard Harris Barham, *The Garrick Club* (New York: privately printed, 1896), p. 42.
21. Marsh, *J. H. R.: Poetry and Prose*, pp. 12–13.

During some of his free time, Reynolds kept in touch with an old friend in Shropshire, John F. M. Dovaston, who had been his father's student in Shrewsbury School.[22] Dovaston was a lawyer who showed his affection for his London friends by including in *Fitz-Gwarine, with Other Rhymes* a sonnet to John and "Lines to Mrs. Reynolds of Lambeth with a Goose." Reynolds returned the affection with an "Ode to Friendship, Inscribed to J. F. M. Dovaston of West Felton" in the *Gentleman's Magazine* for 1812, his first known poem, and later in 1814 dedicated his much more ambitious *The Eden of Imagination* to him.

As early as 1798 one John Dovaston of West Felton (presumably the father of J. F. M. Dovaston) had founded the Breidden Society near Shrewsbury for the purpose of celebrating an annual festival on Breidden Hill with eating, drinking, smoking, poetry reading, toasting, singing, dancing, and—if the record is to be believed—much kissing sparked by the traditional kissing of a stone.[23] Until his death in 1808, John Dovaston conducted the summer festival every year without any formal organization. In 1809 Thomas Yates, who succeeded as president, arranged for written rules, which were recorded by J. F. M. Dovaston. Every year thereafter the president named his successor for the following year before leaving the hill, and "the president's will being by him signified" was "in all cases [to] be held decisive law." But the president had to pay for those prerogatives since he alone was "at the whole Expence, and Trouble of providing a plain cold dinner; Rum, Brandy, and Beer." No laurel being available in the area, a poet laureate could not be created; instead, the abundant fern on the hill led to the substitution of the august position of poet ferneat, a post which vied in importance with that of queen of the hill, which the president filled by solemn pronouncement each year after selecting from the fair revellers. J. F. M. Dovaston was president, poet ferneat, and recorder in 1810; vice-president and poet ferneat in 1811; and poet ferneat in 1812.

Although there is no certain evidence, it seems highly probable that Reynolds attended these festivities with his friend Dovaston while he lived in Shrewsbury, until 1806, while the affairs were being conducted by the elder Dovaston, and he may well have come over from London for such happy occasions in

22. Gittings, p. 10.
23. A manuscript book of the constitution, laws, and minutes of the society is in the Houghton Library at Harvard.

later years. In 1813 Reynolds himself served as poet ferneat, as the following extract from the minutes reveals:

> July 12, 1813
> The day was fine and the company numerous. At one o'clock upwards of sixty sat down to dinner, soon after which the usual convivialities began. The annual tribute of the Poet Ferneat Mr John Hamilton Reynolds of Lambeth was received with heartfelt applause, and he being absent his cup was crowned with the Ferne.

The poem which Reynolds sent shows that he was familiar with the customs of the occasion:

The Reflections of Mirth,
On the Eve of the Breidden Festival, for the Year 1813.

To Morrow's dawn shall scarcely light
The ferny brow of Breidden's height,
   Ere souls of wit and worth
Will rise to sip at Pleasure's rill,
And to make that *"heaven kissing hill"*
   A *kissing* hill of *earth.*

That morn shall find each roseate streak
Reflected bright in many a cheek,
   It's light in many an eye:
The gladsome smiles of day shall grace
The festive scene, and many a face
   Will shine as brilliantly.

Wit and song the scene shall crown,
I the corpse of Care will drown,
   And give the wine a zest.
The sun shall view the gen'rous feast
When first he rises in the east,
   And when he leaves the west.

Time shall throw aside his scythe then;
Time shall bless the feast of Breidden,
   While gay the gambols pass;
Time shall lose his grating pow'r,
Shall disregard the *sandy* hour,
   And only use the *glass.*

Then quickly fly, ye shades of night,
And quickly come, O morning bright,
    In all thy colours fair;
Every lov'd one, every friend,
Around my favour'd circle blend,
    While I support the chair.

John H. Reynolds

Occupying the chair which his poem, read in absentia, supported was Henry Langley, president of the society for that year. The punning evident in the poem, which Reynolds loved all his life, culminated in 1825 in *Odes and Addresses to Great People*, written jointly with Hood. Perhaps it is not too obvious to explain that the "favour'd circle" of the next to the last line refers not only to his many friends in the society gathered for the occasion, but to his wine glass, which he knew would be ceremonially crowned with fern. The reference anticipates happily the many years of convivial imbibing which he would enjoy, but also unhappily the very heavy drinking of his last half-dozen years.

Like Lamb, whom he knew well, Reynolds continued with his clerical duties and produced literary work in his spare time. After following Dovaston's lead by submitting several pieces to the *Gentleman's Magazine* in 1812 and 1813, he expanded to more ambitious efforts in 1814. Through the publishing firm of his friend John Martin, he issued *Safie, an Eastern Tale* in an attempt to capitalize on the vogue of Byronic Oriental tales in verse. Byron was favorably impressed with the book, as can be seen from the entry in his journal, his letter to Reynolds, and his letter to Francis Hodgson recommending a favorable review. Not only did he make these efforts to encourage the author and foster the book; he also met personally with Reynolds over "a vegetable dinner."[24] Later in the same year Reynolds published, again through Martin, *The Eden of Imagination*, an elaborate imitation of Wordsworth, chiefly in the manner of *An Evening Walk*. Martin's short-lived periodical the *Inquirer* also furnished him with an outlet for several poems and prose pieces.

His satisfaction with these promising early achievements was clouded darkly late in 1814 by the death of an unidentified girl whom he loved, a tragedy over which he grieved repeatedly in

24. *Selected Prose*, p. 252. This was the only logical time for the meeting between them which Reynolds reported.

numerous poems dating from January 1815. But in late 1815 he had recovered sufficiently to take several steps up the journalistic-literary ladder by joining the staff of John Scott's influential *Champion*, an association which he continued through December 1817. He increased the volume of his production markedly during these years with a steady flow of literary essays, theatrical reviews, and verse, including, aside from his abundant contributions to the *Champion*, *An Ode* (1815) on the overthrow of Napoleon published by Martin.

Perhaps it was through his publisher, John Martin, that Reynolds met Benjamin Bailey and James Rice, Jr., since Martin's sister married Bailey's brother.[25] Rice, two years older than Reynolds, was a junior attorney in his father's London office; Bailey, three years older than Reynolds, was a serious young man with strong moral and religious inclinations and a "loquacious pen" (as he described it) who resided in London where he had come from his native Cambridgeshire. Rice, whose bad health remained chronic, traveled often to Sidmouth in Devon for relief. In the summer of 1814, he took with him his new friend Bailey, and there the two first met Mary, Sarah, and Thomasine Leigh.[26] A warm friendship developed quickly with the sisters and their cousin Maria Pearse, who spent much time at their home, Slade Hall. Visiting them at Slade about a dozen times from 1814 to 1817, and meeting them at least once at Clifton near Bristol, Rice and Bailey established close bonds with all these "adopted sisters," to whom they supplied abundant verse and glowing prose celebrations of friendship. Bailey fell in love with the youngest, Thomasine, and waxed most sentimental about his adored "Zilia," but she never returned his love, and he came to realize that she was not just displaying maidenly modesty. In 1817 she settled the matter finally by marrying Lieutenant John Carslake of the Royal Navy.

Two of their friendly projects may give some of the flavor of their intimate association. In the spring of 1815, they planted six sweetbriars in the garden at Slade to commemorate their reunion and to represent their growing friendship. In March of the same year, after reading and copying into commonplace books

25. Gittings, p. 12.
26. Clayton E. Hudnall, "John Hamilton Reynolds, James Rice, and Benjamin Bailey in the Leigh Browne–Lockyer Collection," *Keats-Shelley Journal*, XIX (1970), 13 (hereafter cited as Hudnall).

Wordsworth's "Poems on the Naming of Places," they made a walking tour of the coast, naming six rocks of the Dunscombe Cliffs for each of the group and adding a seventh "Union Rock" to symbolize their closeness.

By 25 March 1815 Eliza Powell Drewe from Exeter had joined the group. Bailey was considerate in easing her into this "very dear circle of friends" when she at first imagined that he "thought lightly of her" as an outsider.[27] Despite a certain ponderousness and stiffness of manner, Bailey emerges from the voluminous records as a rather attractive person. Though usually more sentimental or moral than gay, he was capable of high-spirited congeniality. Rice emerges as a man who refused to permit recurring illness to repress his warm affection, his lively wit, and his playful teasing and joking.

Thanks to Clayton E. Hudnall's admirable study of the Leigh Browne–Lockyer Collection, an old error has been corrected, and we now know that Reynolds did not join Bailey and Rice in their visits to Slade during the first two years. The first date by which we can be certain that Reynolds had met Bailey was 18 February 1815, when Bailey wrote a poem on his introduction to Reynolds's sisters,[28] but the two young men may have known each other for some time before Reynolds introduced his friend to the family. The first recorded date by which Reynolds knew Rice was 17 June 1815, the date in a book presented by Reynolds to Rice, who in turn presented it to Thomasine Leigh.[29] It seems virtually certain, however, that Rice, who was so close to Bailey, would have met Reynolds soon after Bailey did, if indeed it was not Rice who preceded Bailey as Reynolds's friend.

Bailey and Rice sang the praises of this young published poet whose two 1814 volumes had been reviewed rather widely and favorably, and the Leigh girls were so impressed that they welcomed any of his verses which they could secure for their commonplace books. In October and November 1815 Rice and Bailey wrote two letters from London which describe vividly the kind of life that they and Reynolds were living at the time. The three frequently spent their evenings together after Rice had finished his legal duties and Reynolds his clerical work. First Rice on 9 October 1815:

. . . when the Evening closes in & we "stir the fire & wheel

27. Ibid., p. 17.   28. Ibid., p. 18.   29. Ibid., p. 38.

the sofa round and draw the curtains close" when "we retire the world shut out."[30] Then it is that We Bailey Reynolds & myself in all the luxury of mental relaxation indulge our fancies our feelings & our humors, & without any of the prescriptions of form, ramble over the fields of imagination running after every butterfly subject that starts up before us.—You will of course suppose that he [Reynolds] is no stranger to our delightful & dear Sisterhood of Slade—but do not therefore for a moment think that we profane your names to those to whom you ought to be Strangers or in whose actual acquaintance we are not confident you would be pleased.—We have always some project on the carpet, some game ever afoot—Either Reynolds or Bailey have ever got the Muses Spur in their side that will not allow them rest or respite—& very sad things their productions *may* be for ought I know—but they give up pleasure & make us every now & then cry "excellent" & that serves our turn you Know as well as if they were better. Reynolds has made progress in a Tragedy that according to my own judgment (if it be not particularized) bids fair to stamp his name with very current reputation.— Within this week too we have bethought of us turning that delightful little tale of Louisa Venoni[31] into an Opera for which it has ever seemed to me admirably suited—I have bargained to furnish the plot & some of the humour & Reynolds the serious & sentimental—or as a Satirist would quiz it, he is to be the Quack & I the merry Andrew of the Piece—no matter if these Our Plans never come to anything or change once a month like the Moon, like her too they serve to enliven our Nights whilst they *do* last.—[32]

Then on 24 November 1815 Bailey described their joint composition of a poem to celebrate Sarah Leigh's birthday:

I told you in my letter of yesterday that we kept or were to keep your birthday at my rooms. . . . On the other side is our *playfulness of affection* [the poem]. Reynolds late in the Evening regretted that we had not sooner thought of writing

30. Cf. Cowper, *The Task*, IV. 36–37.
31. By Mr. M'Kenzie in the *New Novelist's Magazine*, 1786, pp. 151–55.
32. Hudnall, pp. 31–32.

a Poem on the occasion in *triplets* Each person writing a line. . . . I therefore immediately produced the paper, and wrote the first line. . . . They were all written in whirl-winds of laughing. For it was our delight so to change the thought of the person who wrote last as to puzzle him to convert it into anything like agreement or sense with his own, and then to laugh and make what noise we could to interrupt the unhappy artist who was doomed to scratch his head for a thought. . . . I wish you could see Reynolds whose lines are so superior in this little thing to ours—[33]

Toward the middle of 1816, when *The Naiad* neared publication, Reynolds felt secure enough to abandon his clerical work at the Amicable Assurance Society. After Taylor and Hessey issued the poem in August, he left with Rice for a long vacation in Exeter and Sidmouth. During the visit at Slade Hall from 31 August through 11 September, he met the Leighs in the company of Eliza Powell Drewe of Exeter, whom he later married. His letters to Benjamin Robert Haydon reveal that he did not, as has long been supposed, meet Eliza through the Leighs. When he wrote Haydon on 26 August, five days before the visit to Slade, he already knew the Drewes. He was evidently visiting in their house in Exeter; he certainly knew them well enough to ask Haydon to send his letters to their address.[34] He had probably met Eliza and her family through the Drewes' London relative, Mrs. Butler, a friend of the Reynolds family in Lambeth.[35]

Proud of *The Naiad: A Tale with Other Poems*, which combined imitation of Scott and Wordsworthian overtones in the title poem, with Wordsworthian influence even more apparent in the short pieces, he sent the revered Wordsworth himself a copy for judgment. With candor and directness, veiled only thinly by concern for the young poet's feelings, Wordsworth replied with considerable censure and only limited praise. Reynolds must have been disappointed.

33. Ibid., p. 34.
34. See p. 4 below.
35. Gittings, p. 11, reports the friendship of the Reynoldses and Butlers and states that the Butlers had lived in Lambeth. Eliza's father and brother George (and presumably also her mother) having died before the wedding to John, Mrs. Butler represents for Eliza's side "The Head of the Family" in Hood's progress celebrating the wedding (Shelley, p. 325); she was therefore especially close to Eliza.

His disappointment over Wordsworth's letter was more than compensated for by the greatest good fortune from another direction, as he welcomed Keats into the circle which included Haydon and Leigh Hunt. By the time of his return from the vacation in Devonshire, his friendship with Haydon was well established. Although he admired the painter's achievements and expressed his admiration enthusiastically, he was not overawed by the older man's towering ambition and immense confidence in his own ability, as the mock attack and joking tone of much of the two letters he wrote from Exeter reveal. In October 1816 he spent a great deal of time with Hunt and with Haydon, whose temporary quarters at 7 Pond Street, Hampstead, allowed him to visit constantly with Hunt. After Charles Cowden Clarke introduced Keats to Hunt in the week of 13 October[36] and Keats presented Hunt with the sheaf of selected poems as a sample, Reynolds was one of those friendly critics among whom the poems circulated for judgment, as can be seen from Haydon's verses to Reynolds.[37] Aware of his own ability, and ambitious as he was for *The Naiad*, a copy of which he had already sent Hunt, he saw immediately that Keats's poetic potential was clearly superior to his own, and he told Haydon so forthrightly. He could not be envious of one whom he sensed at the outset as the greatest poet of his generation. Furthermore, he was immediately attracted by the extraordinary personality of Keats the man: he dined with Keats at Haydon's in Hampstead on 20 October 1816 and with Keats at Hunt's on another evening in October.[38] From that beginning developed the friendship which was to be Keats's closest outside his family for the next remarkable three years.

Soon Reynolds introduced Keats to his family, who by 22 November 1816 had moved from Lambeth to 19 Lamb's Conduit Street, where Keats visited them often. George Reynolds continued his service of more than seven years for Christ's Hospital, a position which he combined with that of writing master to the Female Asylum in Lambeth. After he was appointed head writing master in 1817,[39] he moved in early 1818 to one of the

36. On the much discussed question of the date of the first meeting, Robert Gittings has the last, and I believe accurate, word in *John Keats* (Boston: Little, Brown, and Co., 1968), p. 83.

37. Hyder E. Rollins, ed., *The Keats Circle*, 2d ed., 2 vols. (Cambridge, Mass.: Harvard University Press, 1965), I, 4–5 (hereafter cited as *KC*).

38. Gittings, *John Keats*, pp. 92–93.

39. Mann, "The Reynolds Family," p. 6.

master's houses near Christ's Hospital in Little Britain.[40] Like Haydon before him, Keats was quickly welcomed by Reynolds's sisters; on 9 March 1817 he wrote of the "kind sisters." He was understandably more attracted to the older girls, Jane, twenty-six, and Mariane, twenty, than he was to the younger sisters. For almost two years he was thoroughly sympathetic, writing them gay and affectionate letters, while they reciprocated by entertaining him in their home and preserving drafts of his poems in their commonplace books. In October 1818 a reaction against their sentiment which had been accumulating climaxed in his disapproval of their jealous treatment of Mrs. Reynolds's niece, Jane Cox, and during his last months in England he was infuriated with both mother and daughters because of their disapproval of Fanny Brawne. But none of this later dislike of mother and sisters seriously affected his close friendship with the son and brother.

Through Reynolds, either directly or indirectly, Keats met most of the other friends who are now such familiar members of the Keats circle. By 17 March 1817 he knew Charles and Maria Dilke, and through the Dilkes he met Charles Brown. By about 12 April 1817 a transfer had been arranged from Keats's unsatisfactory first publisher to John Taylor and James A. Hessey, Reynolds's friends who had published *The Naiad*; significantly, Keats wrote his first letter to Taylor and Hessey from the Reynolds house. Before he left for the Isle of Wight on 14 April 1817, he had met Rice, and about the same time he met Bailey, when the sudden death of a friend brought him to London from Oxford, where he had matriculated on 19 October 1816 to read for holy orders. Keats called John Martin friend by August 1817 and saw him frequently thereafter. Through either Reynolds or Taylor and Hessey, he met Richard Woodhouse, to whom our debt is very great for preserving so much Keatsian material.

Reynolds's services to Keats are so familiar as to require only summary here. He stimulated Keats's writing of *Isabella*, *Robin Hood*, the espistle *To J. H. Reynolds, Esq.*, and numerous short pieces. His discussions and correspondence evoked some of Keats's finest letters on poetry. He championed Keats's reputation vigorously, reviewing *Poems* of 1817 and *Endymion* favorably, encouraging sympathetic reviews from others, and preventing him from publishing the first brash preface to *Endymion*. Throughout the friendship Reynolds was clear-sighted and unselfish. Though

40. Shelley, p. 326.

Hunt had praised Reynolds equally with Keats and Shelley in the
"Young Poets" article in the *Examiner* of 1 December 1816,
Reynolds never confused his own great talent with his friend's
genius. He wrote Keats prophetically, "Do *you* get Fame,—and I
shall have it in being your affectionate and steady friend."[41] The
same modest disavowal of hope for fame appeared also in "The
Pilgrimage of Living Poets," in "Farewell to the Muses," and in two
fine sonnets in *The Fancy*.

Despite Reynolds's diffidence, the association with Keats
stimulated his own work, as he continued to produce a large
volume of material for the periodicals, and at the same time wrote
the poems which went into *The Garden of Florence and Other
Poems* (1821). Probably because he had resolved on marriage to
Eliza Powell Drewe in 1817 (Keats does not speak of an engagement
until 13 July 1818, but he treats it as a matter long settled[42]), he
turned to a steady source of income to replace the salary from the
clerical work which he had resigned the preceding year. Rice
encouraged him to enter law, generously paying for him the fee of
£110, and promising to take him in as a partner if he ever succeeded to his father's business—a promise which he fulfilled faithfully.[43] On 4 November 1817 Reynolds became an articled pupil
in the office of Francis Fladgate, a relative of Rice, and thereafter
divided his efforts between literature and the law in such a fashion
that both his interests eventually suffered. He vacillated between
objection to the dreariness of the law and interest in it: five months
after his entry Keats is obviously replying to his complaints about
the law when he reassures him that all knowledge, including even
dull civil law, has value,[44] but after another year Keats reports,
"Reynolds is completely limed in the law: he is not only recon-
cil'd to it but hobbyhorses upon it."[45]

During the three years after his entry into law, Reynolds's
resolution to concentrate on it was partially thwarted by recurring
illness and partially broken by heavy contributions to periodicals
and by other writing. He wrote for the *Yellow Dwarf*, the *Alfred*,
Constable's *Edinburgh Magazine*, and the *Edinburgh Review*. His
reputation rose to such a height that William Blackwood went to

41. See p. 13 below.
42. Hyder E. Rollins, ed., *The Letters of John Keats*, 2 vols. (Cambridge,
Mass.: Harvard University Press, 1958), I, 325 (hereafter cited as *Letters*).
43. Marsh, *J. H. R.: Poetry and Prose*, pp. 21–22.
44. *Letters*, I, 276–77.
45. Ibid., II, 78.

surprising lengths to seduce him away from his liberal friends. On a visit to London Blackwood sought him out: Keats reports that "Blackwood wanted very much to see him—the scotch cannot manage by themselves at all—they want imagination." [46] John Gibson Lockhart flattered him by praising him above Hazlitt: "The only enlivening things in it [Constable's *Edinburgh Magazine*] are a few articles now and then by Hazlitt, and a few better still by a gay writer of the name of Reynolds. . . . Mr. Reynolds, however, is certainly a very promising writer, and might surely do better things than copying the Cockneys." [47] Blackwood's ally in the enemy camp, Peter George Patmore, brought to its climax this campaign to make Reynolds abandon his friends and turn his coat; on 7 April 1819 he wrote Blackwood:

> I dined with Reynolds a few days ago—and talked with him about writing for you—but, as I expected, from his friendship with Hunt and Hazlitt, he has a feeling about the Magazine which prevents him—otherwise I know he would like to do so—for I was pleased to find that he didn't scruple to speak very highly of the general talent with which the work is conducted. He was very much pleased with the liberal offer you made him—to choose his subject and name his own terms. [48]

In the light of Reynolds's financial need and the startling offer to name his own price, it is very much to his credit that he resisted all advances and remained just as determined as Keats not to "Mortgage [his] Brain to Blackwood." [49]

In addition to contributions to periodicals, Reynolds also produced during his association with Keats the splendid parody of Wordsworth's *Peter Bell* on 15 April 1819; a farce entitled *One, Two, Three, Four, Five: By Advertisement* on 17 July 1819, which Robert Gittings has recently suggested may be worthy of revival; the pseudo-autobiographical memoirs of Peter Corcoran called *The Fancy* in 1820; and *The Garden of Florence and Other Poems* in

46. Ibid.

47. John G. Lockhart, *Peter's Letters to His Kin-Folk*, 2d ed., 2 vols. (Edinburgh, 1819), II, 227–28. Published before 19 July 1819, when Sir Walter Scott acknowledged receipt of his copy.

48. Alan Lang Strout, "Knights of the Burning Epistle," *Studia Neophilologica*, XXVI (1953–54), 85.

49. *Letters*, II, 178–79.

1821. Gittings has observed of the last volume what is certainly true, though unremarked before—its similarity in general pattern to the *Lamia* volume. Both include imitations of Boccaccio, which had of course originally been planned for a joint volume. Just as *Hyperion* is a fragmentary major achievement, so *The Romance of Youth* is a fragmentary major effort. Reynolds's sonnets and lyrics correspond with Keats's, though Reynolds's volume has nothing approaching the massive great odes.[50] While this is not the place for extensive criticism of Reynolds's poetry, I would recommend a poem which other critics have passed over. It is not so much the title poem that is successful, nor the earnest *Romance of Youth*, interesting as it is, but *The Ladye of Provence*, which inclines toward the Chaucerian in its curious treatment of the sentimental and macabre (the heroine is tricked by her husband into eating the heart of her would-be lover). Though not so fascinating as *Isabella*, which it surpasses in weaknesses, it is a strange and partially successful poem with just a hint of irony that leaves a teasing question as to precisely what the poet's attitude was toward his material.

While Keats lived, Reynolds reacted against three members of the Keats circle with whom he had initially been very friendly: Haydon, Bailey, and Hunt. These relationships require some consideration.

The two letters from Reynolds to Haydon in this volume complement Haydon's doggerel invitation to Reynolds to dine with Keats[51] to show clearly that by the autumn of 1816 the friendship was strong and unreserved on both sides. Like Keats, Haydon was received into the Reynolds home, as we know from his sending his best wishes to Reynolds's sisters. Reynolds's friendship with Haydon continued unabated as Keats's grew even to surpass it in 1817. But after 28 December 1817 Haydon exploded when Reynolds neither attended the immortal dinner nor gave any explanation as to why he did not attend. Reynolds could not brook that explosion because of Haydon's long history of being highhanded about appointments and other obligations. Although Reynolds's letters to Bailey have not been preserved, it seems a certain inference that Reynolds was in no mood to treat Haydon gently because Haydon had just behaved irresponsibly toward his older and closer friend, Bailey, who was courting his sister

50. Gittings, p. 13.
51. KC, I, 4–6.

Mariane. Haydon had at first made magnanimous promises to accept an impecunious young painter named Cripps as a student without charge, then suddenly turned cool after Bailey and Keats responded to the proposal, and finally insulted Bailey with a "cutting" letter.[52] Though the Cripps affair had been smoothed out, the memory of it must have rankled. When it came to cutting, Reynolds could always give better than he or his received; he was second only to his idol, Hazlitt, in that department. He replied to Haydon with "one of the most cutting" letters Keats had ever seen, blasting all his faults and weaknesses.[53] Though Keats thought Reynolds should have been more tolerant, he conceded that Reynolds was "on the right side of the question." Of course the friendship ended, and the two were never reconciled. With the passage of time, however, Reynolds's anger cooled so that by the time he reviewed *The Conversations of James Northcote* twelve years later he was impartial enough to defend Haydon in part from Hazlitt's printed attack.[54]

The letters from Rice and Bailey to the Leigh sisters quoted above have revealed the high degree of intimacy between Reynolds and Bailey in the early period. After Bailey began his study for the clergy, the close friendship continued undiminished. Keats's extremely high praise of Bailey is matched by Reynolds's praise of him in the *Yellow Dwarf*.[55] Whenever Bailey could get to London from Oxford, he spent much time in the hospitable Reynolds home and became a paragon of all the virtues for the Reynolds women. No subject could be mentioned without mother or daughters dragging in Bailey's name: "If you mentioned the word Tea pot—some one of them came out with an a propos about Bailey—noble fellow—fine fellow!"[56]

Without the sex appeal of Reynolds, Rice, or Keats, Bailey was passionate by nature, "the slave of passion" to use his own phrase,[57] but less likely to be able to satisfy his desires irregularly, and, even if opportunities offered, he could not as a prospective clergyman easily permit himself such misconduct. Older than his friends by several years, he realized, it seems clear, that he needed a wife. He had tried Thomasine Leigh and failed. He turned to an eligible relative of John Martin's and was again rebuffed. Nothing

52. *Letters*, I, 183.   53. Ibid., I, 205.
54. *Selected Prose*, pp. 414–15.   55. Ibid., p. 215.
56. *Letters*, II, 67.   57. Hudnall, p. 25.

daunted, he selected Mariane from the Reynolds sisters and paid his addresses to her. His peculiar combination of piety and passion is revealed by Keats's account of his wooing her "with the Bible and Jeremy Taylor under his arm."[58] After sustained courtship, he made his declaration, but Mariane demurred, either genuinely not in love with him as Keats thought when he reported that she loved him like a brother, or with pre-Victorian delicacy lest she be supposed to leap at a proposal. Bailey failed to play the expected part of patient and determined suitor who perseveres until he wins the heart of the modest maiden. One can hardly blame him much when he recalls that Bailey had been through all that before, pining away for three years until Thomasine Leigh married another. He was not to be frustrated again. He turned swiftly to the sister of a college classmate, found in Hamilton Gleig a woman not disposed to play at cat and mouse, and married her, after making only a stiff bow to rectitude by returning Mariane's letters and requesting the return of his own.[59]

For an ordinary man, all circumstances considered, Bailey's conduct seems perfectly understandable. But the trouble was that the Keats circle had not looked upon Bailey as an ordinary man—they, Keats included, had regarded him as godlike, and now he was revealed to be merely human. Keats was appalled. After thorough examination of the evidence, Rice decided that he would break with Bailey entirely. Reynolds must have been equally indignant over the supposed callousness to his sister. The sequel to the story, however, shows that neither Keats nor Reynolds was adamant. After time had calmed tempers, Keats wrote to congratulate him on his marriage, and when Bailey came down to London in 1820, Reynolds met him and talked with him.[60] It speaks well for Reynolds's character, as well as for Keats's, that he did not harbor an unrelenting grudge. Mariane did not suffer any serious damage; within a few years she fell in love with her future husband, H. G. Green, and was no doubt happier than she would have been if she had married Bailey and migrated to Ceylon.

Quite friendly with Leigh Hunt early in his career, Reynolds paid him an enthusiastic compliment as a poet in a footnote to *The Eden of Imagination* (1814). On 7 April 1816 he presented him

58. *Letters*, II, 67.
59. Ibid., II, 66.
60. *KC*, I, 232.

favorably in "The Pilgrimage of the Living Poets to the Stream of Castaly."[61] When he visited the Leigh sisters in September 1816, he respected Hunt enough to copy in a commonplace book Hunt's manuscript sonnet before it was published.[62] During the first year of his friendship with Keats, he spent much time socially in Hunt's company, exchanged complimentary sonnets with him, and was grateful, we can assume, for Hunt's high praise in "Young Poets." On 10 September 1817 Reynolds's attitude toward Hunt shifted when he met Hunt in the pit at Drury Lane, where he had gone to review for the *Champion* and Hunt for the *Examiner*.[63] When he told Hunt that Keats was progressing toward the completion of four thousand lines of *Endymion*, Hunt replied possessively: "Ah! . . . had it not been for me they would have been 7,000!"[64] Since he was still very close to Haydon, Reynolds's sympathy had been deflected away from Hunt by Haydon's quarrelling with him. Haydon had warned that Hunt was jealously seeking to preserve the idea that Keats was his protégé, and now Hunt's statement confirmed Haydon's assertion. Reynolds wrote Keats at Oxford of the incident, whereupon Keats conjured up an image of the scene in the theater, "I think I see you and Hunt meeting in the Pit,"[65] and launched into combined disparagement and praise of Hunt.

Thereafter Reynolds's attitude toward Hunt increased in antipathy. Although but one of his letters to Keats has survived, it is easy to understand why so many of Keats's attacks on Hunt were written to Reynolds: Keats was sure that Reynolds would be a receptive reader. Reynolds did not abandon his own liberal views —he contributed to John Hunt's *Yellow Dwarf* and he allowed Leigh Hunt to reprint his defense of *Endymion* in the *Examiner*— nor did he compromise his political principles by writing for the Tory press, but he sensed the danger to Keats's literary reputation posed by continued association in the public mind of Keats's name with Hunt's, and he sought to prevent it. He remonstrated successfully against a plan for publishing *Hyperion* in a joint volume

61. *Selected Prose*, p. 48.
62. Hudnall, pp. 20–21n.
63. *Letters*, I, 162, 169. Files of the two newspapers reveal the date and place. Reynolds wrote no review for 7 September 1817. For 14 September 1817 Reynolds and Hunt reviewed the same performance, and both mention attending on the same night, 10 September.
64. Ibid., I, 169.
65. Ibid., I, 162.

with a work by Hunt.[66] When he reprinted the revised version of the early "Pilgrimage of the Living Poets" in 1820 as "Living Authors: A Dream," he quietly omitted the favorable treatment of Hunt, compensating only slightly by adding in a footnote condescending praise of the *Indicator* as "a very clever little periodical work."[67] Even more strongly than Keats, he reacted against Hunt's personal traits, writing John Taylor of "the vain and heartless eternity of Mr Leigh Hunt's indecent discoursings" and of "the irksome, wearing consciousness of a disgusting presence, than which I know of nothing more dispiriting."[68] It is not surprising that Reynolds's savage private attacks cloaked by public civility left Hunt so baffled that he wrote Hazlitt, "Reynolds is a machine I don't see the meaning of."[69]

Many years later Charles Cowden Clarke, who remained unswervingly loyal to Hunt, noted that "Reynolds poisoned him [Keats] against Hunt—who never varied towards Keats."[70] But that remark is only a partial truth; Clarke's love of Hunt led him to overstate the case. Reynolds reenforced a change in Keats's attitude, as Keats realized for himself Hunt's limitations and weaknesses.

After Reynolds's death, Charles W. Dilke wrote from general recollection that "in every number of the London the traces of his light and pleasant pen were visible."[71] The new letter to John Scott in this volume refines upon Dilke's memory by showing the date and circumstances of Reynolds's beginning his contributions, as well as identifying the long two-part essay "On Fighting" in his best lively and jocular manner.

As a contributor to the *London*, he became involved indirectly in the duel which led to the death of its first editor, John Scott, and he and Rice served as attorneys for Scott's second, Peter G. Patmore, in the legal action that followed. After Taylor and Hessey acquired the magazine in 1821, for three and a half years he assisted with the editing and wrote most of the theatrical reviews, epistolary articles under the pseudonym Edward Herbert, other literary articles, reviews of current books, and poems. Although

66. See p. 66 below.
67. *Selected Prose*, p. 256n.
68. See p. 22 below.
69. Percival P. Howe, *The Life of William Hazlitt*, 3d ed. (London: Hamilton, 1947), p. 291.
70. *The Novello–Cowden Clarke Collection* (University of Leeds, 1955), p. 9.
71. *Athenaeum*, 27 November 1852, p. 1296.

Dilke's statement that these years were "the only true period of his literary life"[72] is inaccurate because it neglects his achievement during Keats's lifetime, it serves to emphasize the success he enjoyed with the *London*. He published prose worthy to be printed along with the greatest prose geniuses of the period, Lamb and Hazlitt, and he joined Lamb, Hazlitt, Thomas De Quincey, Bryan Waller Procter, John Clare, and other contributors at the convivial dinners given by John Taylor.

His long-delayed marriage to Eliza Powell Drewe on 31 August 1822, accompanied by the jubilation of many old members of the Keats circle as can be seen from Thomas Hood's comic progress to celebrate the event, led to many years of domestic happiness. Though he had lost Keats, he gained Hood, who married his sister Jane in 1825, and the second literary friendship flourished too.[73] What life was like in the Reynolds home at this time can best be seen in a passage from Hood's letter to Mrs. Reynolds about January 1823 when he was engaged to Jane:

> I shall need all my strength if you expect me to come and romp with your grandchild [Eliza Reynolds Longmore's baby]. My dear Jane writes that owing to Mr. Acland's delay, it is likely that they may not come up till the week after next. Pray make use of the interval in double-bracing your nerves against "the little sensible Longmore." She will put you to your Hop-Tea. I expect she will quite revolutionise Little Britain. The awful brow of Mariane, the muscular powers of Lottie, the serious remonstrances of Aunt Jane, the maternal and grand-maternal authorities will be set at naught with impunity. As for Green [Mariane's suitor] and I, we shall come up empty about dinner-time, and in the hubbub, be sent empty away. The old china will be cracked like mad; the tour-terelles, finger-blotted and spoiled; the chintz—now *couleur de rose*—all rumpled and unflounced! . . .
>
> Think of your good and clever daughters, who paint sea nymphs, and sing, and play on the piano; and of your son John, dear to the Muses. I think few families have been

72. *Notes and Queries*, 4 October 1856, p. 275.
73. For detailed accounts of the Reynolds-Hood relationship, see Alvin Whitley, "Keats and Hood," *Keats-Shelley Journal*, V (1956), 33–47, and Peter F. Morgan, "John Hamilton Reynolds and Thomas Hood," *Keats-Shelley Journal*, XI (1962), 83–95.

dealt with so well, if, indeed, any. There's Jane, and Eliza, Mariane, and Lottie,—four Queens; and John,—you must count "two for his nob."[74]

The scene here depicted supplements Keats's more fragmentary references to suggest the appeal of this cultured and hospitable home five years before to John, George, and Tom Keats, Rice, Bailey, Woodhouse, and Charles and Maria Dilke.

When he left the *London*, Reynolds's comic and satirical gifts continued, first in a sparkling attack on John Wilson in the *Westminster Review* and then in his greatest popular success in 1825, *Odes and Addresses to Great People*, the work produced anonymously with Hood which Coleridge was certain that no one but Lamb could have written. From 1828 through 8 June 1831 he owned part of the *Athenaeum*, but he unfortunately sold his share to protest Dilke's cutting the price in half. He must have regretted that step sorely as Dilke's judgment proved sound and the magazine prospered, while his own financial situation grew ever more desperate. He managed, however, to supplement his income from law by contributing steadily to the *Athenaeum* through 1837; as pedestrian as much of that work was, he deserves credit for leading Dilke's campaign against the corrupt puffing of new books. Theatrical writing also augmented his income: to the operetta *Gil Blas* of 1822 and the Mathews monologues of the twenties, he added in the thirties Fanny Kelley's *Recollections* (1830), *A New Entertainment* (1833), and *Confounded Foreigners* (1838).

The Garrick Club, which he joined as a charter member in 1831, provided an opportunity to meet socially with Thackeray and Richard Harris Barham, both of whom sought to assist him in placing his work in periodicals. The new Garrick Club letters in this volume display some small but attractive facets of his character. He shows his solicitousness for Eliza by ordering special meat for her in her illness. He reveals his kindliness toward the old porter, whom other members wanted discharged because of senility, by requesting that he be given the convenience of a chair and a rug.

After more than a decade of family harmony in his close and happy association with Hood, in 1835 Hood quarreled bitterly

74. Shelley, pp. 329–30. For non-cribbage players, the nob is the jack, held in the hand, of the same suit as the card turned up. It counts one in the game; Hood shows his admiration for Reynolds by doubling his nob. Keats occasionally called him Jack too.

with the Reynolds family, as Jane lay desperately ill. Although Hood specifically excepted Reynolds from the angry blasts that he fired at the other members of the family, Reynolds must have been sorely grieved by this family friction. In the same year his life was darkened further by the death at the age of ten of his daughter, Lucy, the only child surviving after the death of an infant years before.[75]

On 26 October 1838 a long history of financial difficulties resulted in a certificate of bankruptcy. The increasing need for money pressed him to cease contributing to the respected *Athenaeum* and to turn instead to the less dignified but more lucrative *New Sporting Magazine*, which he edited through 1840. After long service as Hood's attorney, he was dismissed in 1841, and that abrupt action probably marked a break in the old friendship.[76] During his last decade, he clung precariously to the small prestige of a free-lance author by contributing to *Ainsworth's Magazine*, the *New Monthly*, and *Bentley's Miscellany*. The letters to Richard Bentley, new in this book, identify another series of essays in the *Miscellany*, including copious paraphrases of Latin verse, though neither prose nor verse is superior in quality to his late work which has long been known.

Abandoning private legal practice in 1847, he secured a position as assistant clerk of the county court at Newport in the Isle of Wight, where he spent his last five years. Having procrastinated his own life of Keats for twenty-five years, he was pleased to cooperate enthusiastically with Richard Monckton Milnes in preparing the first extensive biography. In other respects his last years were gloomy. Although Lord Ernle may have exaggerated somewhat in calling him "a broken-down, discontented man . . . whose drunken habits placed him beyond the pale of society,"[77] since he did function responsibly and earn the respect of many in the Isle of Wight,[78] it is clear that he drank heavily and that he was usually unhappy and depressed before he died on 15 November 1852. Lord Ernle meant to damn him by charging that he went to his grave a "professed . . . Unitarian and a bitter Radical," but for that integrity Hazlitt would have been

75. *KC*, I, cxxi.
76. Morgan, "John Hamilton Reynolds and Thomas Hood," pp. 90–91.
77. Rowland E. Prothero, Lord Ernle, *The Works of Lord Byron, Letters and Journals*, 6 vols. (London: John Murray, 1898–1901), III, 46n.
78. Willard B. Pope, "John Hamilton Reynolds, the Friend of Keats," *Wessex*, III (1935), 3–15.

proud of his old comrade on the *Yellow Dwarf* in the campaign against autocratic kings and self-serving prelates.

The Letters

Of the fifty-eight letters and fragments of letters printed here, twenty-one have been reprinted from Hyder E. Rollins's *The Keats Circle*, the classic work which in this century has been most influential in fostering research of the group of minor writers and friends who surrounded Keats. Twelve have been republished from a wide variety of periodicals, ranging from the *Gentleman's Magazine* of 1812 through the London *Times* of 1928 to the *Keats-Shelley Journal* of 1970. Eight (counting as one the fragment quoted by Keats) have been printed in books, covering a span of time from *The Papers of a Critic*[79] in 1875 to Maurice B. Forman's edition of *The Letters of John Keats*[80] in 1952. Seventeen are published in this volume for the first time.

The time has arrived to gather all Reynolds's letters which are recoverable into one readily accessible place. They have been so widely scattered in place and time that even those with a great interest in Reynolds have overlooked them. So indefatigable and successful a researcher as George L. Marsh, on whose solid foundation all later studies of Reynolds have been built, never chanced to see two of Reynolds's longest and, in some ways, most interesting letters, which were buried in an appendix to *The Memoirs and Correspondence of Coventry Patmore*.[81] Even Hyder E. Rollins, whose resourcefulness and thoroughness are not likely to be equaled, did not happen to find the one letter to Francis Jeffrey which had been printed inconspicuously in a week-day issue of the London *Times*.

Many of the published texts, furthermore, were inaccurately edited from manuscripts which still survive. The originals now in the Princeton University Library show that Basil Champneys's version of the letters to Patmore omits a thirty-three-word sentence and makes numerous other, smaller errors, some quite significant, such as the slip which conceals the identity of John

79. Sir Charles W. Dilke, 2 vols. (London, 1875).
80. 4th ed. (London: Oxford University Press, 1952) (hereafter cited as Forman, *Letters of Keats*).
81. Basil Champneys, 2 vols. (London: Bell, 1900) (hereafter cited as Champneys).

Scott's ally against *Blackwood's* by printing "Mr. Cullock" for "Mc Cullock" (John Ramsay McCullock). Or for a less drastic yet meaningful example, the generally better edited *Bookman* version of the letter to Thomas Hood [82] obscures the sense of a sentence by printing as "Commissioner Tim" what the manuscript in the Bristol Central Library reveals to be "Commissioner Lin." Though the host of errors can be understood in the light of changing editorial standards, it is desirable to have texts which are accurate. Except for the letters reprinted from *The Keats Circle*, which I have reproduced exactly from that text, I have edited directly from the manuscripts in all cases where I have been able to locate them.

Of course these fifty-eight letters are only a small fraction of those which Reynolds wrote during his lifetime—just an average of one for each year of his life. It is especially unfortunate that we have but one full letter to Keats, because Keats regularly burned old letters and papers. Tom Keats's endorsement of that well-known "Do you get fame" letter, "Reynolds to John," suggests that the only reason we have it is that Tom was so gratified by the high tribute to his brother that he took special pains to save it. That is a deservedly famous letter, of course, but it probably was not typical of the tone of Reynolds's letters to Keats. Reynolds was being solemn about a matter that was a grave conviction with him, his firm belief in Keats's great genius from which he never wavered throughout his life, as can be seen from his proud declaration to Richard M. Milnes twenty-eight years later that Keats "had the greatest power of poetry in him, of any one since Shakespeare!"[83] The one letter to Keats was probably not typical also for another reason: Reynolds was unusually subdued in it because he believed that he had renounced any major effort to write great poetry himself. We can guess from the character of Reynolds that emerges from his letters to others, as well as from the depictions of his character by John Clare and Hood, that most of his letters to Keats resembled the tones of his jovial and high-spirited letters to Benjamin Robert Haydon, his long, bantering letter to John Taylor, and his one animated letter to Hood.

It is just as regrettable that the numerous other letters which he must have written Hood over the years have not been pre-

82. Dated 13 March 1840, first published in the *Bookman*, LXIV (September 1923), 277–78.
83. See p. 59 below.

served. The mysterious difficulty with Hood in the 1840s, whatever its nature may have been, was doubtless the cause. Eliza Reynolds's refusal to furnish the Hood children with Hood's letters to Reynolds when they were preparing *The Memorials of Thomas Hood*[84] evidently stemmed from the hostility of intimate friendship turned sour, a bitterness which had not died after more than a decade. If the Hood children suppressed or destroyed Reynolds's letters to Hood in retaliation, one can hardly blame them for being human enough to seek revenge, but as a result the world has almost certainly lost a number of fine letters.

In general I have followed the editorial procedures of *The Keats Circle*. Shaped brackets (⟨ ⟩) enclose cancellations. Square brackets ([ ]) are employed for illegible words, for words or letters inserted because they are necessary for the sense and were omitted by mere oversight, and for a question mark to indicate a doubtful reading. Curly braces ({ }) are used for editorial insertions to fill lacunae; where three dots are enclosed ({. . .}), they indicate a gap which is explained in a footnote. Three asterisks (* * *) at the beginning or end of a letter indicate that part is missing. Flourishes on signatures have been ignored. All postscripts, no matter where placed in the letter, are included at the end. Sources of the letters, addresses, and postmarks are recorded in headnotes. In the main Hyder Rollins's footnotes have been borrowed intact for the letters reprinted from *The Keats Circle*, though I have made a few changes to adapt them to this book. For example, since *The Keats Circle* preceded Rollins's definitive edition of Keats's *Letters*, he cited M. B. Forman's fourth edition; I have changed all those references to Rollins's edition of *The Letters of John Keats*.

It is a pleasure to thank the following persons and institutions for permission to reprint the letters indicated: the President and Fellows of Harvard College for the Reynolds letters from *The Keats Circle*; the Pierpont Morgan Library for the four letters from the Morgan manuscript; Willard B. Pope for the letters to Haydon from Haydon's manuscript diary; William R. Maidment, Borough Librarian, and the Libraries and Arts Committee of the London Borough of Camden for the letters to Mary Leigh from the collections at Keats House, Hampstead, used by permission of the Libraries and Arts Committee of the London Borough of Camden;

---

84. Frances Freeling Hood Broderip and Tom Hood (Boston, 1860).

Signora Vera Cacciatore of the Keats-Shelley Memorial House at Rome for the manuscript of the letter to James A. Hessey of March 1818(?); Sir Geoffrey Keynes for the letter to John Scott; the Princeton University Library for the manuscripts of the letters to Peter G. Patmore; the Harvard College Library for the letters from the Garrick Club Papers and the letter to Richard H. Barham, used by permission of the Harvard College Library; the University of Illinois Library for the letters to Richard Bentley; the Henry E. Huntington Library for the letters to P. F. Laporte, reproduced by permission of the Huntington Library, San Marino, California; the Bristol Central Library for the manuscript of the letter to Hood; and the Yale University Library for the manuscript review of John Clare and the letter from Allan Cunningham to Reynolds. I am also indebted to Peter F. Morgan for directing me to the letters to Bentley, and to Clayton E. Hudnall for the help provided by his excellent study of the Leigh Browne–Lockyer Collection.

List of Letters

LIST OF LETTERS

APPENDIX

The Letters of
John Hamilton Reynolds

The Letters of
John Hamilton Reynolds

1

TO THE *Gentleman's Magazine*
5 December 1812

Published in the *Gentleman's Magazine*, vol. LXXXII, pt. 2 (supplement for 1812), p. 607.

Dec. 5.

Mr. Urban,

In the first volume of Miss Seward's Poetical Works, edited by Walter Scott, esq.[1] there are some extracts made from her literary correspondence. In one of these, p. 79, she mentions having received great delight from an Ode which her mother was accustomed to recite to her in her childhood; but that she never could learn the author of it, having heard it from one who was not possessed of literary curiosity enough to inquire its origin. As there is no note upon the subject, it is probable that the Editor is also unacquainted with the author. In looking over a volume of old poems lately, I discovered it inserted amongst them, and ascribed to Anne, Countess of Winchelsea, who lived in the reign of Queen Anne.

The second stanza is thus printed in Miss Seward's Works:

> "How pleasing the world's prospect lies;
> How tempting to look through!
> Parnassus to the Poet's eyes,
> Nor Beauty, with her sweet surprize,
> Can more inviting shew."

But in the volume I have mentioned, it is inserted in the following manner:

> "How pleasing the world's prospect lies;
> How tempting to look through!

Not Canaan to the Prophet's eyes,
Nor Pysgah, with her sweet surprize,
Can more inviting shew."[2]

Miss Seward's version certainly possesses more poetical beauty, though perhaps the latter one is most correct. The Ode in general is very excellent, and is written in that style of chaste simplicity which was so peculiar to the Poets in the reign of Anne.

Yours, &c.
J. H. R.

1. Anna Seward, Poetical Works of Anna Seward, with Extracts from Her Literary Correspondence, 3 vols. (London 1810).
2. "Life's Progress," lines 6–10.

2

TO BENJAMIN R. HAYDON

26 August 1816

ALS: Inserted in the diary of Haydon, now owned by Willard B. Pope of Burlington, Vermont, whose excellent edition of it has revealed the artist fully: The Diary of Benjamin R. Haydon, 5 vols. (Cambridge, Mass.: Harvard University Press, 1960–63). First printed in the Keats-Shelley Journal, VI (Winter 1957), 98–99.
Address: B. R. Haydon Esq./ 41 Great Marlboro' Street. Postmark: Exeter/ 26 Au 26/ 1816 [in the second blurred postmark, only 1816 is legible].

My dear Haydon.

You were in bed, you know, the other night, when I called, —and what is more you were very drowsy and very dull,—in short you had nothing of the Haydon about you, that I could discover. If you had been one of the waking, I should have explained to you what I wished you to do with Wordsworth's letter[1]—& all about the matter. But pouring information over you, was, at this sleepy hour, of no more service than parliamentary oratory, or than talking to the Elgin Marbles & waiting for an answer. Now will I enlighten you. In about a week you will receive two copies of my Poem, with the most momentous inscription. One of these you will keep for yourself, as a trifling but sincere mark of my friendship for you, & of my sense of the friendship—which you hold for me. You will find little said,—but you may rest satisfied that it is sincerely felt. Long dedications are often sickly in their flattery—& generally dull in their composition. Besides my inscription will not occupy much of your illustrious time.[2] The second copy you will convey, with the letter I wrote, to Wordsworth;—And if you would give my friend the Naiad ⟨an intro⟩ a letter of introduction, I should be glad.—I am in no great humour for letter writing—and this scrawl may likely turn you into that state in which I left you. I want some tremendous fillip—some descent of a Rogero on his winged horse—some thundering blow with his sword,—some meeting with Polyphemus,—some desperate ghost story—some anything to rouse me to high thoughts and heroic atchievements.

Devonshire is a glorious Country. I do not wonder that you gentry excel in the fine Arts. Painting and Poetry seem to me to grow with the grass—& bloom with the flowers—& breathe from the Hills around here. You would deserve to be excommunicated if you did not throw a lustre over your name, with such a birth-place. Why, Immortality must hold its court here—and Fame walks about the fields like a common personage.

I caught a cold while travelling,—a plague for your Coaches. Night airs are faithless friends—they say pretty things to one's face, & cut one during their flattery. How is your swelled face?—I will exchange a very pretty sore throat for it.

Do write to me—if you can. I know you *can*, but I am not so sure that you will. Tell me all the news about Literature & the Fine Arts. Recollect for the act of writing to me—this charitable act—you will obtain innumerable benefits here and your name will be put up in the Capital—Children of the 20^h Century shall lisp it ⟨your name⟩ in a National Gallery—your pictures shall be squabbled for by turbulent Emperors of future ages;—they shall deck a better Hall than the Louvre. You shall grow green in poetry—& music shall hallow you. You shall walk in Paradise—& eat apples without any danger. Honours shall be heaped upon you. Will you not write now?—I wish my paper would let me tell you what punishments would fall on you, if you do not write.

3

The weather is sunny and settled;—And I am determined to be happy. Farewell.

Yours while this machine is to him.—
J. H. Reynolds

Mond. morn g^3
My Direction.
Mr Reynolds
at———Drewe Esq^4
South Street
Exeter

1. One by Reynolds to Wordsworth, left with Haydon to accompany Reynolds's recently completed *The Naiad*. Haydon had known Wordsworth for over a year, but Reynolds had not yet met him.
2. *The Naiad* was dedicated to Haydon.
3. 26 August 1816.
4. Reynolds was visiting at the home of W. Drewe (died before 1818), whose daughter, Eliza Powell Drewe, he married on 31 August 1822.

3

TO BENJAMIN R. HAYDON

28 September 1816

ALS: In the diary of Haydon, owned by Willard B. Pope of Burlington, Vermont. First printed in *Keats-Shelley Journal*, VI (Winter 1957), 99–100.
Address: H. T. Haydon Esq./ 41 Great Marlbro' Street/ London. *Postmarks:* Exeter/ SE 28 [*rest blurred illegibly*]; A/ 30 SE 30/ 1816.

Exeter. Sat^y. Evening. 1816

My Dear Haydon.

Thanks for your letters. Why they were Cartoons in the way of feeling and Enthusiasm—they ought to be hung up in a Gallery of Letters, which should be erected for the display of our national literature. Your observations, my dear fellow, on your feelings as relating to your glorious art,—are all of a piece with the forms on your canvass:—They leap out of the heart, or burst full and perfect from your brain. They tell of the deepest feeling and the richest enthusiasm. The letters of a Painter (I speak of Painter here,—as you have taught me to comprehend it in the largest sense) are noble, when they are unlaboured and generous, and spirited. But you will think I have put down my claim to the title of Poet,

4

& have taken up that of Flatterer:—But remember what Hamlet says to Horatio about friendship & flattery,[1]—and then think of me accordingly. Talking of Poetry,—I must now thank you for your *good taste*, as Sir Fretful would call it,[2] in praising my verses, & being satisfied with the dedication. You have much gratified me, by informing me of Mrs. Montague's[3] good opinion, of whose taste I have so often heard so much. The Book is at any rate a well dressed One. The Naiad is a truly respectable woman as far as personal appearance goes:—I shall leave it to the world to decide on the beauty of her voice & the fascination of her Song. I wish some of the Critics may be lured into an admiration of her,—if she could but charm with her warblings, the bony heart of a Scotch literary Surgeon,[4]—what might not be looked for at my hands, & in my hopes. If the Naiad is to be ⟨hacked⟩ dissected;— Heaven knows what complaint, the Operator may say occasioned her decease. But I will not talk of death now,—nor of the damnation which may tread on the heels of it—"We know the End will come,—& there's an End." I am glad you have sent the Copy to Wordsworth for me:[5]—Oh Haydon when I think of the sunlike genius, & fine firm principle of that Noble Poet;—I think higher of human nature, of the age in which I live. He is the Milton of our day. He has twined the pillars of the Temple of Philosophy with the loveliest flowers of Poetry. He has turned by the touch of his genius, the mountain air of his country into words. Liberty breathes through his Poetry, as the wind wanders over his Hills. Thought is the friend of his retirement. I long to see Wordsworth. —And am I to be read in Italy?—Am I to go into the land of soft suns & polished hearts:—where Painting & Poetry dwelt, as in their home?—I shall envy my own Child. What would I not give to roam down the banks of the Arno, with a volume of Shakespeare or Spenser in one hand, & with your arm to support my other. How should we read! How should we think! How richly sho^d. we talk! The landscape lying like a mixture of grass & gold about us—The blue sky arching over us.—flowers at our feet— and water running through smiles and music beside us. Why illustrissimo Pittore! We should feel like Raphaels and Spenser. We should think of elder times,—of romances—of fairy wonders! —We should speak up to the pitch of a Titania or an Oberon. Surely our Spirits would be fit company for the wildest & lightest Spirits that ever revelled on the bank of moonlight-stream, or crept into a harebell to screen them from a hot sunrise.—Well—

So much for a freak of the fancy. Castle building is a glorious business,—and I know of no one who could like to be apprenticed to the trade, so well as myself.—Farewell.

Yours for ever.

J. H. Reynolds

My name is J. H. & not S. W.[6]

If you write by RETURN OF POST I shall get it here. Pray do, & tell me all the news.[7]

1. *Hamlet*, III.ii.62–79.
2. In Sheridan's *The Critic*, I.i.245–49, Sir Fretful Plagiary praises the judgment of those whom he expects to approve his play.
3. Mrs. Basil Montagu. See below, pp. 29, 32n., for Reynolds's later warm friendship with her.
4. Francis Jeffrey. Reynolds's hope was frustrated. The *Edinburgh Review* ignored it, though various minor periodicals praised it.
5. Wordsworth answered Reynolds's letter on November 28, mixing considerable censure with limited praise (*The Letters of William and Dorothy Wordsworth: The Middle Years*, ed. Ernest de Selincourt, 2 vols. [Oxford: Clarendon Press, 1937], II, 158–59).
6. Haydon evidently confused J. H. Reynolds with another Reynolds whom he had met. Samuel William Reynolds was an engraver who produced the "Head of a Girl" used by Hazlitt as the title-page vignette for *Liber Amoris* (*The Complete Works of William Hazlitt*, ed. Percival P. Howe, 21 vols. [London: J. M. Dent and Sons, 1930–34], IX, frontispiece). In jocular retaliation, Reynolds addressed this letter to "H. T. Haydon."
7. This second postscript was written on the back flap. In his diary, opposite the page on which he pasted the letter, Haydon wrote, "I paid him no such compliment." Haydon probably added that remark after his bitter quarrel with Reynolds in December 1817; in later years he frequently looked back through his diary and inserted comments.

4

TO BENJAMIN R. HAYDON

22 November 1816[1]

ALS: In the diary of Haydon, owned by Willard B. Pope of Burlington, Vermont. Printed in Forman, *Letters of Keats*, p. 11n.

Lambs Cond[t] Street
Friday morng 10 oClock

My Dear Haydon,

As you are now getting "golden opinions from all sorts of men,"[2] it is not fitting that One who is sincerely your Friend should be found wanting. Last night when you left me—I went to my bed—And the Sonnet on the other side[3] absolutely started into

my mind. I send it you, because I really *feel* your Genius, &
because I know that things of this kind are the dearest rewards of
Genius. It is not equal to anything you have yet had, in power, I
know;—but it is sincere, & that is ⟨som⟩ a recommendation.
Will you, at my desire, send a copy to Mʳ Keats, & say to him,
how much I was pleased with his.[4]

Yrs affectionately
J H Reynolds

Sonnet to Haydon

Haydon!—Thou'rt born to Immortality!—
I look full on;—and Fame's Eternal Star
Shines out o'er Ages which are yet afar;—
It hangs in all its radiance over thee!
I watch whole Nations o'er thy works sublime
Bending;—And breathing,—while their spirits glow,—
Thy name with that of the stern Angelo,
Whose giant genius braves the hate of Time!
But not alone in agony and strife
Art thou majestical;—Thy fancies bring
Sweets from the sweet:—The loveliness of life
Melts from thy pencil like the breath of Spring.
Soul is within thee:—Honours wait without thee:—
The wings of Raphael's Spirit play about thee!

J. H. Reynolds[5]

Novʳ 1816.

1. Undated, but the Friday in the heading was clearly the one immediately
after Wednesday, 20 November, when Keats wrote *To Haydon*: "Great spirits
now on earth are sojourning."
2. Cf. *Macbeth*, I.vii.33.
3. *Sonnet to Haydon*, which Reynolds published in the *Champion*, 24 November 1816.
4. *To Haydon*: "Great spirits now on earth are sojourning."
5. Underneath Haydon wrote years later: "Wild enthusiasm B. R. Haydon
1842."

5

TO MARY LEIGH

28 April 1817

ALS: In the Keats House at Hampstead, published by the permission of
William R. Maidment, borough librarian and curator, and of the Libraries and

Arts Committee, London Borough of Camden. First printed in Hudnall, pp. 29–30. See this article (pp. 11–39) for an excellent account, which corrects many earlier errors, of the relationship of Rice, Bailey, and Reynolds with Mary (1793–1876), Sarah (1794–1845), and Thomasine (1796–1883) Leigh, their cousin Maria Pearse, and their friend Eliza Powell Drewe.

Address: Miss Leigh/ Slade Valley/ near Sidmouth/ Devon. *Postmark:* Ap/ 28/ 1817

19 Lamb's Cond[t] St. 28th Apl. 1817

My Dear Mary.

All those base-born terms which the gallant hearted Hal lavished so laughingly on merry old Falstaff, are due to me for my delay,—and though their appliances to me would be feeble as far as personal appearance goes, yet would they be strictly attachable on the score of sloth, and neglect.—But I am accusing myself unfairly,—and merely, I believe, for the sake of revenging myself upon an allusion to my favourite Poet. I like to begin with some word to, or recollection of Shakespeare,—right divine: to pluck a lovely feather from the fairy wing of his Imagination, and deck the ⟨fool's⟩ cap of my letter with it. His name, surrounded as it is with the unquenchable light of perfect fame, shines on the vacant waste of my Paper, like a cloudless sun at mid-day glowing on Salisbury Plain. His pen is the key with which we unlock the gates of all Ancient Cities, and wander ⟨and⟩ among Tribes, and become familiarized with all the olden manners. By his aid, as Aladdin was by the Magician's, we are led through the magnificent chambers of the earth, and see evergreen Plants & Trees, and ever fresh fruit, and pluck jewells from [illegible word canceled] all things around us. There is surely a congress of all the noblest beings of the most majestic nations assembled in his works, speaking a language true to the veriest "thoughts of Nature," and catching at, & scattering [illegible word canceled] on earth ⟨thoughts⟩ fancies truely etherial.—But I am becoming *essaical*, (the everlasting fault of my letters) and what is more, tedious and *prosaical*. You will say of me, as Iago says of himself, that "I am nothing, if not critical."[1]—However I will here release you from this needless eulogy on Shakespeare, which you could so well enter into without its being expressed, and become more letteral. I have been long resolving to write to you, and as long neglecting my resolution. Various causes,—important & imperative as far as concern myself, but which could not interest you,—have prevented me from paying that attention to you, which even good manners demanded, had there not been a higher voice,—that of friendship,—calling

upon me. That I have shamefully delayed,—I honestly admit,—
and sincerely ask your pardon.

Last night I passed the evening with our friend Rice, and in
a way which of all others is the one nearest to my heart,—in conversation on tasteful & happy & domestic subjects. George
Drewe[2] and Bailey (who is suddenly called up to London by the
death of a Friend)[3] made up our party. We were all as comfortable
as man ought to be;—that is—delightfully quiet and conversational.—On Thursday last Hazlitt was with me at home, and
remained with us till 3 o'clock in the morning;—full of eloquence,
—warm, lofty & communicative on every thing Imaginative &
Intelligent,—breathing out with us the peculiar & favourite
beauties of our best Bards,—Passing from grand & comma[n]ding
argument, to the gaieties & graces of wit & humour,—and the
elegant and higher beauties of Poetry. He is indeed *great* company,
and leaves a weight on the mind, which "it can hardly bear." He is
full of what Dr. Johnson terms "good talk." His countenance is
also extremely fine:—a sunken & melancholy face,—a forehead
lined with thought and ⟨living with⟩ bearing a full & strange
pulsation,—on exciting subjects,—an eye, dashed in its light with
sorrow, but kindling & *living* at intellectual moments,—and a
stream of coal-black hair [illegible word canceled] dropping around
all. Such a face, so silent and so sensitive, is indeed the banner of
the mind. "It is as a book, in which men may read strange things."[4]
He would have become the pencil of Titian, and have done justice
to the soul-fed colours of that bold & matchless Italian. I fear you
will be tired with this long *personality*, but I remember having read
a few papers of his to you, and therefore imagine that you will not
be wholly uninterested in him. What a fine hour was that in your
room with Eliza, Maria & yourself!—Do you remember it?—I
have not forgotten a single slope, brake, or tree, which feasted my
eyes when I was sojourning at your green, romantic & sea-crowned
home. There was that delightful walk on the mellow Autumn
evening, under the young trees, to the cliff!—There was the Sea
"whispering eternally on desolate shores"![5]—There was the ruin,
with its ivied window, and silent story of decay! There was the
blessed sky, with its wide look of peace, and the calm smile on its
face!—But "above all," there was the company of Eliza & yourself. I know not how it is, Mary, but that evening is sweeter to me
apparently in recollection. It seems something hallowed by
memory. I remember all—Eliza with her handkerchief over head,

9

by my side,—& you, with yr. brow "bared to the elements."—
Well, such days might come again! Will you remember me kindly
to your family,—not omitting yr. Brother. As Eliza and Anne[6] are
staying with you, I think it would be but respectable to *extend the
remembrances to them.*—You will not, I trust, treat me, as I have
treated you,—but shame me with a speedy charity. Do Sarah &
Tamsine like Spenser?—I hope they do. They must,—for he is
the second Poet[7] to Shakespeare. I wish I was now ⟨m⟩ with you
to read his glorious & chivalrous Tale. If I can I will put a few of
my ideas of Spenser into an essay, that you may see why I think
so highly of him. Milton is more studied & less natural,[8] more
enormous in his language, more sounding—but his wings are not
of such dazzling brightness. He does not set us dreaming on fairy
feasts & forms. He does not carry us about in the company of all
that is splendid and innocent. No.—I have by this, I conceive,
pretty well tired you—& therefore conclude with putting my
name to the title of Friend

J. H. Reynolds

1. *Othello,* II.i.118.
2. The brother of Reynolds's future wife. He died in December 1818. See
Letters, II, 15.
3. From Oxford, where Keats visited him several months later. The friend
who died is unknown.
4. Cf. *Macbeth,* I.v.60–61.
5. An adaptation of Keats's "It keeps eternal whisperings around/ Desolate
shores" from "On the Sea," which Keats first sent Reynolds in a letter of 17
and 18 April 1817 (*Letters,* I, 132).
6. Eliza's younger sister.
7. Here an X directs the reader to a corresponding X on the flap beneath
the address.
8. Here a *Λ* directs the reader to a corresponding *Λ* on the brief space at the
top of the first page.

6

TO MARY LEIGH

1817(?)

ALS: In the Keats House at Hampstead, published by the permission of
William R. Maidment, borough librarian and curator, and of the Libraries and
Arts Committee, London Borough of Camden. Only the last page of this
undated letter has been preserved. Someone has written at the top "one sheet

only." That it was addressed to Mary is inferred from Reynolds's request in the last paragraph that his respects be paid to Sarah and Tamsine. Since the "Anne" on the seal is probably Eliza Drewe's younger sister, Reynolds may well have written from Exeter. The date is a guess.

Address: Miss Leigh/ Slade Valley.

so lately had tossed their madness over. We will sit together,— and read,—in the glorious Shakespeare, whose mind was the atmosphere of the world,—that visited all things,—or the Eternal Temple of thought,—or the garden of Fancy,—and the breath of Nature:—We will read,—if you chuse the rather,—in that next best Bard,—the sacred & the serene hearted Milton.—We will talk of many pleasant and summer-born subjects.—We will walk —look at the sea—listen to the trees—& the playful waters.— I know that my character must suffer in your estimation (to speak seriously, for I am, I know not how, in my mind) by this word, which must remain an unredeemed pledge in [illegible word canceled] your hand:—But I cannot avoid it—and I must trust to Time to lend me an opportunity of refreshing my name in your recollections. Will you write to me while I yet stay here?—

Give my affectionate regards to Sarah & Tamsine and say to them that I will some day trouble them with a line or two,—if so I may. My very best respects and thanks to Mrs. Leigh.

Your affectionate Friend

J H Reynolds

7

TO JAMES A. HESSEY

March 1818(?)

ALS: In the Keats-Shelley Memorial House at Rome. Printed in Forman, *Letters of Keats,* pp. 119–20n.

Thursday

Dear Hessey

I am confined to my room, with a heavy cold & fever, leading a life of pain, sleeplessness & bleeding.

Could you, to beguile the time, lend me Hazlitt's first lecture[1] to read over—unless it is in hand, or at the Printers—I will return it to night. I am as low, as bad company. Have you a proof of Keats' Poem[2] for a body.

Yours truly

J H Reynolds

I believe I must take Wordsworths leech gatherer into keeping.

1. Taylor and Hessey published Hazlitt's *Lectures on the English Poets* (1818).
2. *Endymion.*

8

TO JOHN KEATS

14 October 1818

Reprinted from *KC*, I, 43–44. Partly printed by Sir Sidney Colvin, *John Keats*, 3d ed. (London, Macmillan, 1920), pp. 312–13, and Amy Lowell, *John Keats*, 2 vols. (Boston: Houghton Mifflin, 1925), II, 105–6, and almost entirely in Forman, *Letters of Keats*, pp. 223–24 (which followed the W. H. Arnold sale catalog of May 1901). Two sentences are quoted in *Harper's New Monthly Magazine*, LV (1877), 361, and the whole letter, then owned by Arnold, is printed in the *Century Magazine*, L (October 1895), 953.

Address: Mr John Keats/ N° 1 Well Walk/ Hampstead. *Postmark:* 4 o'Clock OC. 14 18 {18}; Two Py Post Unpaid EOStrand.

My Dear Keats

I was most delighted at seeing you yesterday,[1]—for I hardly knew how I was to meet with you, situated as you are, and confined as I am. I wish I could have stayed longer with you. As to the Poem I am of all things anxious that you should publish it, for its completeness will be a full answer to all the ignorant malevolence of cold lying Scotchmen and stupid Englishmen. The overweening struggle to oppress you only shews the world that so much of endeavour cannot be directed to nothing. Men do not set their muscles, and strain their sinews to break a straw. I am confident, Keats, that the Pot of Basil hath that simplicity and quiet pathos, which are of sure Sovereignty over all hearts. I must say that it would delight me to have you prove yourself to the world, what we know you to be;—to have you annul the Quarterly Review, by the best of all answers. When I see you, I will give you the Poem, and pray look it over with that eye to the *littlenesses* which the world are so fond of excepting to (though I confess with that word altered which I mentioned, I see nothing that can be cavilled at)—And let us have the Tale put forth, now that an interest is aroused. One or two of your Sonnets you might print, I am sure—And I know that I may suggest to you, which,—because you can decide as you like afte {rward. You} will remember that we were { . . . }² together—⟨but⟩ I give over all intention and you ought to be alone. I can never write anything now—my mind is taken the other way:—But I shall set my heart on having you, high, as you ought to be. Do *you* get Fame,—and I shall have it in being your affectionate and steady friend. There is no one I am more interested in—and there is no one that I have more pleasure in communicating my own happiness to. You will gratify me much by letting me have, whenever you have leisure, copies of what you write;—for *more than myself* have a sincere interest in you. When shall I see you—& when shall I go with you to Severn's

Your ever affection {ate}
J. H. Reynolds

Wed^y Morn^g

1. Lowell, *Keats*, II, 105, says that Reynolds visited Keats "on Thursday, October thirteenth," carried off the manuscript of *Isabella*, and wrote this letter "the next morning." But it is dated Wednesday and postmarked October 14. The thirteenth was Tuesday. The letter is endorsed by Tom Keats, "Reynolds to John."

2. Lowell has "we were [to] pu [t out]"; Colvin, "we were to print." The *Century* reads, "[Nobody] will remember that we were [to write]."

9

TO JOHN TAYLOR

12 January 1819

Reprinted from KC, I, 72–74.
Address: Mr Taylor/ Taylor & Hessey/ Booksellers/ Fleet Street/ London.
Postmark: Illegible.

Dear Taylor

Will you excuse the trouble I am about to put you to?—The following advertizement I am desirous of having inserted in the Times, with the reference, if not disagreeable, to yourself. It is for the young Man of whom I once spoke to you, & who really is too good for so dense a city as this. He is very desirous of quitting it—and seeing "foreign parts" and I am sure his qualifica-

13

tions are such as to make him a desirable companion to any given young Gentleman in want of a clever and well informed associate. He knows all that the advertizement holds out—and more to boot. His direction is "Henry Worsley, Manly's Buildings, St Sidwell Exeter"—This is all the information you can require—as on application he will be ready, like Mr Croker's potatoes, to speak for himself.[1] I inserted it in the Times once with no effect, and therefore, as in all lotteries, I am tempted by the bad success to venture again. I make no apologies for troubling you thus, because I know your readiness to assist in any act of kindness:—If you would send it the day you get this, I should be obliged. TO PERSONS GOING ABROAD. A young Man aged 25 years, of respectable con-nexions wishes to accompany any Gentleman as a Companion to the Continent. He understands the French Language thoroughly, has a knowledge of music and of painting;—has been accustomed to sketching. He is also possessed of other acquirements which might be found useful in such a Situation—Address by Letter (postpaid) to H. W. at Taylor & Hessey Booksellers Fleet Street.[2]

The above I think will do, and a reference to a Bookseller looks more tempting to the eyes of the little-Learned. If you can do anything among your Friends or Customers it would be so much kindness carried to my account:—Though I do not think your interest lies much amongst the pretty Gentlemen that escape from College[3] to Continent.

I expect to be home—indeed I am sure, that I shall return, —by Saturday, when I will repay you for all but the trouble of this little task.—The Weather here is as changeable as a Woman (this is in the established style of manly comparison,—and therefore I adopt it.)—The sun now is as bright as though it had forgotten the Month, an{d} had put on its August Coat and Waistcoat. But I must also tell you; not to make you Envious of our Devonshire Suns, which are a ray or two better than most County Suns,—that we have decent allowances of frost & rain, at handsome intervals. —And last night the Wind was so high, one might as well have lived in a pair of bellows with one's face to the snout.

I am much bounden to you for the Coat, which behaved in a truely friendly manner all the way down here,—you could not have taken greater care of me yourself. Remember me to Hessey,— and make my Compts to Mrs Hessey. If you see Keats tell him I

14

am well, & not forgetful of him. I suppose by this,—you have received from Hilton a sketch for the Poem. I shall like to see it. Ever yours most sincerely

J H Reynolds

Exeter[4]
12 Jan[y] 1819

1. Hazlitt, in the *Liberal*, July, 1823 (*Complete Works*, XX, 113), tells how Croker was introduced to Horace Smith, Prince Hoare, Richard Cumberland, and others, and how ''he began to make a display of his native ignorance and impudence on all subjects immediately, and no one else had occasion to say any thing. When he was gone, Mr. Cumberland exclaimed, 'A talking potato, by God!''' Hazlitt elsewhere (ibid., XII, 101, 183n.) mentions ''this '*talking potatoe*''' and ''A certain *Talking Potatoe*.''

2. The advertisement appeared in the *Times*, Saturday, January 16, p. 1.

3. Perhaps Henry Worsley came from Oxford University. The name Worsley, from an Isle of Wight family, frequently turns up there.

4. In December Keats wrote: ''Lately George Drewe expired in a fit—on which account Reynolds has gone into Devonshire'' (*Letters*, II, 15).

10

TO JOHN KEATS

September(?) 1819

Only this extract from the letter has been preserved because Keats copied it into a letter of 21 September 1819, *Letters*, II, 210–11. Keats seems to have copied from a letter recently received so that the month of Reynolds's letter was probably September.

* * *

I am glad to hear you are getting on so well with your writings. I hope you are not neglecting the revision of your Poems for the press: from which I expect more than you do

* * *

11

TO JOHN SCOTT

14 March 1820

ALS: In the collection of Sir Geoffrey Keynes, by whose generous permission it is published.

Address: J Scott Esq

Dr Sir

Our Friend Horace Smith[1] applied to me to write for your magazine—I declined becoming a regular Correspondent then from a fear that my leisure would not allow it. I now however send you an article or two—of a light kind—as you seem to need such the most. I fear you will not be able to use the lines on the Ship, though the time has elapsed enough I sho^d think to deaden their application.[2] If the whole packet does not suit you, I will thank you to put a cover over it & have it left at my house soon.

Yours &

J H Reynolds

Little Britain
14 March 1820

I understood from Smith the remunerat^n to be 10 gu{ine} as a sheet I had intended to send these to the Edinburgh Magazine but that work is so heavy & dull, that I am sick of it.[3]—And they can but go there, if they do not suit a London.

1. Horatio Smith (1779–1849), but always called Horace. Reynolds had known him at least since 1816 when they both wrote for John Scott's *Champion*. Smith had earlier recommended Reynolds as a contributor to the *London* in an undated letter to Scott (MSS 1706, f. 189, National Library of Scotland; extract quoted in Josephine Bauer, *The London Magazine, 1820-29*, in *Anglistica*, vol. I [Copenhagen: Rosenkilde and Bagger, 1953], p. 62n.). See below, p. 25, for Reynolds's interview with Smith after the Scott-Christie duel.

2. This letter makes possible the identification of Reynolds's first work for the *London*. It was "On Fighting. By a Young Gentleman of the Fancy," I (May 1820), 519–22, and I (June 1820), 640–45. Reynolds wrote "an article or two" because it was rather long and Scott did decide to split it. By "lines on the Ship," Reynolds meant the passage in "On Fighting" where he argued that men and creatures should not be mismatched: "It would be like . . . feeding the Boa Constrictor a live goat (as is recorded by Mr. Macleod of the Alceste), or any other act equally authentic and abominable" (I, 522). On 18 March 1816, the *Alceste* struck a reef in the Gaspar Strait and was wrecked irrecoverably. The crew escaped to Gaspar Island, where they were beset by Malays and exposed to serpents. The catastrophe is described in John M'Leod, *Voyage of H. M. S. Alceste* (London, 1818). Reynolds was apologetic for joking about a calamity that had caused great suffering, but Scott evidently agreed that the lapse of four years had tempered readers' feeling so that they would not react unfavorably.

3. "On Fighting" shows strong marks of having been written originally for the *Edinburgh* (or old *Scots Magazine*). Reynolds goes out of his way to set up a mock competition in fostering different sports between the Scots and the English. The article was designed to appeal to both a Scotch and an English audience. See especially I, 520 and 521 (in the latter Reynolds jokingly compares himself with Jeffrey—both lawyer-critics).

12

TO JOHN TAYLOR

March 1820(?)

Reprinted from *KC*, I, 105. The date is a mere guess.
Address: Mr Taylor or Mr Hessey/ 93 Fleet Street.

Dear Taylor

Did you see Keats?—And how is he?—And what is "the cause of thunder"?[1]

Ever yours
J H Reynolds

Wednesday morn^g

1. *King Lear*, III.iv.160.

13

TO JOHN TAYLOR

4 July 1820

Reprinted from *KC*, I, 119–20. The third paragraph is quoted by Lowell, *Keats*, II, 424.
Address: John Taylor Esq/ Messrs Collett & Falkener/ Bath. *Postmark:* JY 4 1820.

50 Poland Street
4 July 1820

My Dear Taylor

You will be astonished at receiving a Letter from me, but pray do not let it see you in those fustian clothes or it may be equally startled at you. The cause of my writing to you is this:— My Father among his various places of *emolument* hold[s] the place of Writing Master to the Asylum[1] & he *has* held it for the last 15 years.—Some of the Managers of this concern are now proposing to lop his trifling salary of £50 per annum down to £30—on the economy *lay*. He has gained great credit by his attention to the children as I am told,—and I really think it hard that he should be the only martyr to the saving system. What I want you to do is to write, if you do not mind such a thing, to Lord Radstock[2] who is a leading & an attending man and get him to oppose this reduction, if on inquiry he finds it causeless. If you could write

17

to him by return of Post, he will get your Ans[r] on Thursday morning, the day of the meeting & decision.

I really would on no account have you write, if it will be thought an obligation and you know that I always thus freely ask you, because I have the confidence in your refusing anything that would be painful, unpleasant or impossible. I have not said a word to my Father of this letter, & therefore your declining on the score of delicacy, will not be known, but of course it would be a pleasure to me to be in anyway instrumental in preserving to him what he is really intitled to, & the loss of which it would be an affectation to say he would not feel. So much for this—

Poor Keats! You cannot think how much pain Hessey's account[3] has given me:—for if ever there was a worthy fellow & clever fellow on Earth—he is that fellow. His Book looks like an Angel, & talks like one too. You have heard of the damn'd Literary Gazette.[4]

What say you to Blackwood?—Is it not clever & apt.—I am & have been really amused with it.[5]

This is no letter—but you, up to your eyes in Sun, want no letters—and my heart strings are just at present, of red tape[6]— Yours ever most truly

J H Reynolds

1. The Female Asylum, Lambeth.
2. William Waldegrave (1753–1825), first Baron Radstock of Castletown, Clare's patron.
3. See Keats's own reference, June 23 (*Letters*, II, 300), to his spitting of blood and Hessey's letters, about the end of June, to Clare (Edmund Blunden, *Keats's Publisher: A Memoir of John Taylor* (1781–1864) [London: Jonathan Cape, 1936], p. 73).
4. On July 1 it mentioned Keats's book (p. 423) "which is on the eve of publication," with one sentence of comment and various quotations from the poems.
5. In June 1820, *Blackwood's* (VII, 294–306), reviewed Reynolds's *The Fancy*, jokingly pretending to accept the pseudonym Peter Corcoran as authentic in the process of praising the book.
6. Referring to the pressure of legal business. The letter was written from Rice's address.

14

TO FRANCIS JEFFREY

13 July 1820

Reprinted from the London *Times*, 30 October 1928, p. 19. The *Times*, explaining that the letter had been placed in its hands by Mr. Gabriel Wells of New York, recorded the address as given here.

THE LETTERS OF JOHN HAMILTON REYNOLDS

Address: Francis Jeffrey, Esq./ Edinburgh, N.B.

Little Britain
13 July 1820

My dear Sir

    I have seen Mr. Proctor[1] since the receipt of your Letter & have informed him on the question of the division of the article—so that we now understand that he is to take the Tragic and I the Comic Drama.[2] If you are better pleased with the arrangement I cannot wish it otherwise. The [?][3] article you shall receive in time certainly,—by the 12th.

    Mr. Keats is young—22 I should think.[4] He was educated for a Surgeon, but has been foolish enough to abandon his profession and trust to his books and a very trifling income left by his Father. He is an orphan. His health is now in the worst state, for as his medical man[5] tells me he is in a decided consumption, of which malady his mother & Brother died. He is advised—nay ordered—to go to Italy; but in such a state it is a hopeless doom. Owing to Leigh Hunt's fatal patronage, Keats' name and fate have been joined with his in the Quarterly and Blackwoods magazine. By his friends he is very much beloved; and I know of no one who with such talents is so unaffected and sincere, or who with rich personal abuse, as he has suffered, could be so cheerful & so firm. His politics are strong against the Quarterly Review. I do not, my dear sir, at all ask you to review his book, unless you are disposed to do it, from reading it, as it were a book put into your hands by a Stranger.

    I am extremely obliged to you for your politeness and kindness in writing to Mr. Brougham.[6] I know not to what works to refer him for a specimen of my style. I wrote in the Champion newspaper during the years 1815 and 1816, when it was in the hands of Mr. Scott; and he might see me there. Or if I should have the pleasure of seeing him I could by other means satisfy him.

    I agree with you quite about Proctor's new Book, with the exception of Amelia Wentworth, which [I] think is written with great simplicity and pathos. The rest of the Book bears marks of haste—and is therefore sketchy and indecisive.[7]

    I know not whether I impinge on your rules, in requesting £40 or £50 on account, and indeed I have written so little hitherto that I can ask it with little grace. But it would be a great

19

convenience to me, and I will take care to write it forthwith. However, I would not have you send it, if you have any objection.

I am ever dear Sir,

Your very faithful and obliged servant,

J. H. Reynolds

[P.S.] Would you like a literary article on Hazlitts 3 last vols. I
have them by me & would write it at once for the next No. if
you wish it.[8]

1. Bryan Waller Procter (1787–1874), perhaps still better known by his
pseudonym, Barry Cornwall.
2. No joint article appeared. Procter wrote "On Tragedy," which was
finally published in the *Edinburgh Review*, XXXVIII (February 1823), 177–208,
but there was no section or article on comic drama.
3. The bracketed query appears in the *Times*.
4. He was three months short of twenty-five. Probably Reynolds exaggerated
his youth to enhance Jeffrey's favor.
5. Dr. George Darling, who first examined Keats on 22 June 1820 (*KC*, I,
lxxv).
6. Henry Peter Brougham, Baron Brougham and Vaux (1778–1868).
7. *Marcian Colonna, an Italian Tale, with Three Dramatic Scenes, and other
Poems* (London, 1820). Jeffrey may have attended to Reynolds's judgment, for in
the review of Procter's book, "Amelia Wentworth" is called "pathetic and
poetical" (*Edinburgh Review*, XXXIV [November 1820], 457).
8. *Lectures on the English Poets* (1818), *Lectures on the English Comic Writers*
(1819), and *Lectures on the Dramatic Literature of the Age of Elizabeth* (1820), none
of which had been reviewed in the *Edinburgh*. This postscript clarifies a hitherto
unexplained complaint by Hazlitt in a letter to Hunt of 21 April 1821: "It was
but the other day that two friends did all they could to intercept an article about
me from appearing in the said E[dinburgh] R[eview], saying 'it would be too
late,' 'that the Editor had been sounded at a distance and was averse,' with
twenty other excuses, and at last I was obliged to send it myself, graciously, and
by main force, as it were, when it appeared just in time to save me from
drowning" (Howe, *Life of Hazlitt*, p. 321). Jeffrey vetoed Reynolds's suggestion,
and Reynolds and probably Thomas Noon Talfourd tried to persuade Hazlitt
that no review would be acceptable. Hazlitt stubbornly sent Talfourd's review
of *Lectures on the Dramatic Literature of the Age of Elizabeth*, and Jeffrey published
it in the *Edinburgh Review*, XXXIV (November 1820), 438–49—doubtless much
to Reynolds's discomfiture.

15

TO JOHN TAYLOR

21 September 1820

Reprinted from *KC*, I, 155–58. Printed in part by Lowell, *Keats*, II, 472–73.
Address: John Taylor Esq/ 93 Fleet Street/ London. *Postmark:* B 23 SE 23
1820.

THE LETTERS OF JOHN HAMILTON REYNOLDS

Exmouth

21 Septr 1820

My Dear Taylor

I do not know when I have been more gratified at the receipt of a letter than now, for you give me the best of news, full to the brim, that Keats is positively off for a better Lungland.— There is no half-measure information of expected departure or promised amendment,—but smack you come down upon me with the *Ultimatum* to Sir John. Your Alphabet commences at Z. Your Letter is in *finals* only. I could find in my heart to discuss the merits of an old wall, which is now stretching along before my eyes in all the stony incorrectness of antiquity,—(and very little of your speculative Ingenuity could wrench it into something Roman)—Or I could go into a slight inquiry, touching & concerning certain derivatives, which should carry us through all your thrice-column'd *tomes*, and all the Volumed Wealth of *Dick Woodhouse*; —if only to shew my sense of your kind & kindly-welcomed letter; —but that I dread the sorrow of your Family,—the decided tone of Hilton's reproof—The austere & chastened remonstrances of that Prelatical Worthy, whose scriptural & saintly visage[1] glooms over the fire place of your little back Oratory:—Indeed Hessey Hilton, Dewint—All would abhor me for touching on a subject which is potent in its mastery over your spirits and in its blanching of the cheek. I resolved however to say something of your darling, dreary, torturing pursuit as a grateful return for your recollection of me—and ⟨try⟩ truly I opine that that one page, as incomprehensible & foggy as becomes the subject, is a full ⟨retur⟩ remuneration ⟨for⟩ to *you* for the time you have expended in my service.

Seriously, my dear Taylor, I am very, *very* much pleased at what you tell me,—and the more so, since Keats has departed so comfortably, so cheerfully, so sensibly. I cannot now but hold a hope of his refreshed health, which I confess his residence in England greatly discouraged, particularly as he was haunted by one or two heartless and *demented* people[2] whose opinions and conduct could not but silently influence the bearings of his Thoughts & hopes. Absence from the poor idle Thing of woman-kind, to whom he has so unaccountably attached himself, will not be an ill thing; And who would not be banished from the vain and heartless eternity of Mr Leigh Hunt's indecent discoursings. I quite pity you the three days visits of that feeble man,—not on account of the ill-conditioned power of his tongue (for I could not wish him a more wholesome medicine than your own good sense) —but for the irksome, wearing consciousness of a disgusting presence, than which I know of nothing more dispiriting. I wonder, I must say, at his asking himself to dinner at *your* Table!—But *dining out* is I conceive, the most rational plan of living for him;— and when he asks himself to another's Board, he does wisely to accept the invitation.—Keats then, by this, is at Sea fairly,—with England, and one or two sincere friends behind him,—and with a warm clime before his face! If ever I wished well to man, I wish well to *him*! I should indeed have liked to have seen him off with you, but Woodhouse & yourself[3] are a Host of friends in your- selves, and he is not unmindful of you, I warrant me, at this moment!

You scarcely tell me enough, I fancy, of the Brawnes, or whether Keats said anything of *them* before he left. They have been really attentive to him, which we should not forget. Severn will much like the voyage, & greatly pleasure Keats, if I mistake not: Though he is scarcely the resolute, intelligent or cheerful com- panion which a long voyage and a sickly frame so anxiously call for. I wish *you* yourself could have cast Fleet Street & Dull Care behind you, and have taken a trip with our ailing friend:—But we must not, as Sancho says,[4] look for better bread than's made of corn!

I am passing a quiet, happy, beneficial holyday at Exmouth, by the side of a very pleasant shore,—in the very eye of the wind, and under some of the finest evening skies that Novel-Readers could desire. Our clouds here are very rich and splendid,—and appear to have *left off* business *as* clouds and to have come to the Sea-side to cut a dash. They throw gold about the sky like dirt. At the same time, I should not forget our blues and our emeralds,— which are better than any colours in a Silk Mercer's or a Jeweller's. To the north of our Habitation, the River Exe stretches along in a noble manner,—and at Sunset, the brilliant and glossy lights, bro- ken by the ⟨the⟩ a remarkably wide shore and relieved by old black boats and shattered vessells, are really of the most beautiful & varying kind. Dewint would qualify for a crown of straw, if he were here; and I have more than once wished for his art to fix imperfectly even on paper the fleeting splendours of the richest skies I ever looked upon.—I could be pleased to smear down some of the "cloudy glories" about me on that rough paper, which I have admired in Dewint's portfolios.—Remember me to Hessey—cum Woodhouse. Is the latter flown?

Yours very faithfully

J H Reynolds

1. A portrait of Taylor's father.
2. Possibly Brown and Haydon, as well as Fanny Brawne and Hunt.
3. Perhaps Taylor did not mention that Haslam had also traveled on the boat to Gravesend (see *KC*, I, 149n.).
4. Peter Motteux's *Don Quixote* (1717), I.i.7. See Apperson's *English Proverbs* (London: J. M. Dent and Sons, 1929), p. 42.

16

TO PETER G. PATMORE

6 March 1821

ALS: In the Princeton University Library. A faulty version, omitting a thirty-three-word sentence and mistaking a number of significant words, was printed in Champneys, II, 420–22. Below the address "J.R." is written in James Rice's hand. Above the address, on the back flap when folded, "7 Marh 1821" is written in an unknown hand.

Address: Mr. P. G. Pitt/ Poste Restante/ Calais. *Postmark*: F 21 98.

50 Poland Street

6 March 1821

My Dear Sir

I ⟨give you⟩ take a large sheet of paper that I may give you as full an account of what has come to my knowledge since your absence, as I am sure you will be desirous of receiving.[1] And first you will receive with this a very full copy of the evidence at the second meeting of the Jury at Chalk Farm, as taken by Mr Rice, which it appears to him was considerably more in your favour than that of the preceding day:—Though as you will perceive nothing transpired before the Coroner to soften the evidence of Dr Darling.[2] Mr Pettigrew is not included in the verdict brought in by the Jury, and he is therefore left to us as a witness, and his evidence will assuredly go greatly in your favour.[3] The Verdict you will perhaps have heard, is such as we expected—"Wilful murder against yourself Mr. Christie & Mr Trail"—And the warrant was issued on the night of the Inquest at about 1/2 past 12. The feeling of the Jury and of the public, is certainly strong against you, being so excited by Darling's Evidence;—to temper this as much as possible, Mr Rice has caused the following paragraph to be inserted in the Chronicle[4] and it shall appear in the Times.[5]—"The Report of the proceedings upon the ⟨late⟩ Inquisition conveying an erroneous impression of the circumstances which attended the late fatal meeting between Mr Scott & Mr Christie; The Public, and particularly the friends of Mr Patmore are requested to suspend their opinion till the proper Investigation takes place, to which Mr Patmore will submit himself."—This is quite as much as need be said to the Public. The Friends of C. & T. have determined to print nothing before the Trial, and therefore the short statement above was obliged to come as from yourself or your Friends. I am informed that a meeting of C's party took place on Saturday, at which Sir W. Scott attended—and it was determined that he should surrender himself at the proper time.[6]—On Saturday Evening I saw Mr Minshull the then sitting Magistrate at Bow Street—And I stated to him that you would appear to take your trial at the fitting period, requesting to be informed whether on such an understanding, all further search would be with held;—Mr Minshull however observed that he could not receive any such communication,—that the warrant was in the officer's hands—And that it was his and their duty to cause you to be apprehended.—We have every reason therefore to be convinced of the propriety of the step which we advised you to take.[7]—Yesterday I had an interview with Mr Baldwin,[8] who the Evening before had see Mrs Scott[9] and conversed with her for a considerable time. She had written a Letter to you, going toward affording you some consolation for the dreadful loss of Mr Scott, and quoting a few words from the letter written by him to her (which I had delivered to Mr Dom. Colnaghi, together with his own, *previous* to the arrival of your letter,—and which has safely reached Mrs Scotts hands) stating that "you had done all you could to prevent a meeting."[10]—This letter of Mrs Scott threw the blame on Trail, whose name occurred twice in it,[11]—on reading which, Mr Baldwin hinted at the propriety of forwarding a written Document of this nature, which you might be compelled to produce as evidence. To this observation, Mrs Scott made the following important reply—"As to producing any letter of mine— there will not be occasion for such a measure, as I shall hold myself quite ready to come forward, if necessary, to give evidence of what I know—And I shall then speak of Mr Trail, as I now write."—These were her words I think, they certainly however

24

convey [her *and an illegible word canceled*] the purport of her communication. Mr B. says that she is quite able to see Mr Rice or myself on the subject and Mr Rice will therefore after Friday (the day of poor Scott's funeral) write a note requesting an appointment.—Yesterday afternoon I dined with Horace Smith at Fulham, and heard from him a minute Relation of the affair, as far as he had any connection with or knowledge of it.[12] He only saw Scott twice on the subject at the first interview S. communicated the message he had received from Mr Lockhart, stating that he had so received it in your presence, and that you offered your services in the affair, which he could not but accept:—That he came to Smith because he considered you were too forward and inconsiderative in the business;—And that he was desirous Smith would take upon himself the arrangement of the dispute. At the second meeting nothing particular occurred and Smith declares that he has no knowledge of any circumstance which could at all favourably affect the question as far as regards yourself. It is highly probable that Scott has given this account of your conduct to Smith in order to excuse an application made to him at second-hand—And indeed this is strengthened by one observation of Smith that when he called and saw you, Mr Scott came to him in the passage & requested him to acknowledge that ⟨you⟩ he had called you in before or written (as I understood) a letter.*[13] However this Evidence does not seem material to your cause, though it shall be well considered;—and if upon getting your statement Mr Rice sees that Smith can communicate or corroborate any material fact, I will see him again, and he is very clear and ready in the business. —I have written to McCullock[14] as poor Scott directed,—and have also sent Circulars to the Magazine Contributors.—

Thus, I have given you all the information you will require —And now, as Mr Rice wishes to add a few wo{rds} I shall close this Letter.—I am—Dear Sir

Yours very truly—
JH Reynolds

[James Rice to Patmore]

My dear Sir,

I am here at Raggetts[15] where I expected to find the Passport ready to [*word canceled illegibly*] be sent along with the other documents—but owing to some misconception as to its importance he has not yet procured it.—I trust he may be correct in supposing it not to be very material to the comfort or safety of your residence in ⟨Paris⟩ Calais I will take care that by the next Post it shall be forwarded without fail—In the meantime if you should be under any local embarrassment or difficulty of any sort for want of it, I am sure that on using my name to my Friend Mr Saurent he will render you any service or assistance in his power c[16] as he is a Merchant of some consequence & influence I believe in the Town I doubt not but that his good word would under such circumstances be advantageous.—At present, it must not be concealed from you that public opinion is at its worst—but even if you were more under the influence of it than I believe you to be, I should in this case bid you be of good cheer, for I am satisfied that your ⟨case is⟩ conduct is much misrepresented & capable of being fully proved to be ⟨see⟩ so—*wait patiently* therefore the appointed time until the change come—I have not time to add more than that I am Dr Sir

Yours very truly
J Rice Junr.[17]

1. After the duel between John Scott and Jonathan Henry Christie (died 1876), the firm of Reynolds and Rice served as attorneys for Patmore. A concise summary of the incidents leading to this letter may be helpful. As a result of Scott's attacks on *Blackwood's* and John Gibson Lockhart in the *London Magazine*, Lockhart directed his London friend Christie to demand an apology. Scott refused, Lockhart came down to London to challenge him, and Scott declined to accord Lockhart the privilege of a gentleman unless he denied the editorship of *Blackwood's*. Lockhart published an account of his case including a denial of editorship, but he sent Scott a copy without the denial. After Lockhart's return to Edinburgh, Scott denounced what he regarded as the duplicity of the differing account. In Lockhart's absence, Christie assumed the quarrel and insulted Scott. Scott challenged Christie, and the duel was fought on Friday, February 16, at 9:00 P.M. by moonlight at Chalk Farm with Patmore as Scott's second, James Traill as Christie's, and Thomas J. Pettigrew (1791–1865) as attending surgeon. In the first fire Scott missed, while Christie leveled his pistol but aimed away from Scott. In the second fire Scott missed again, and Christie shot Scott in the groin. After Scott had been moved to Chalk Farm Tavern, Christie, Traill, and Patmore went into hiding and shortly thereafter fled to France. Despite initial favorable reports, Scott died on February 27. The text of the letters and subsequent footnotes will supply further information on particular details of the duel and its aftermath. For a full account of the duel, see my "The Scott-Christie Duel," *Texas Studies in Literature and Language*, XII (Winter 1971), 605–29. For an account of the trials of Christie and the seconds, see my "Reynolds and Rice in Defence of Patmore," *Keats-Shelley Memorial Bulletin*, XXI (1970), 12–20.
2. Dr. George Darling testified on the first day of the coroner's inquest, March 1, from a memorandum which he had made of Scott's statement to

him between nine and ten o'clock on the morning following the duel, Saturday, February 17: "This ought not to have taken place; I suspect some great mismanagement; there was no occasion for a second fire. All I required from Mr. Christie was, a declaration that he meant no reflection on my character: this he refused, and the meeting became inevitable. On the field Mr. Christie behaved well, and when all was ready for the first fire he called out—'Mr. Scott, you must not stand there; I see your head above the horizon; you give me an advantage'; I believe he could have hit me then if he liked. After the pistols were re-loaded and every thing ready for a second fire, Mr. Trail called out—'Now, Mr. Christie, take your aim, and do not throw away your advantage as you did last time.' I called out immediately, 'What! did not Mr. Christie fire at me?' I was answered by Mr. Patmore, 'You must not speak: 'tis now of no use to talk; you have nothing now for it but firing.' The signal was immediately given; we fired; and I fell." (London *Times*, 3 March 1821.)

It is easy to understand why the public was so incensed against Patmore. Lest the reader be left with an ineradicable bias against Patmore, it is necessary to explain his misunderstanding immediately. He knew that Traill had spoken to Christie, but the remarks were "perfectly unintelligible to him." He had seen Christie level his pistol and had no reason to suppose that Christie had not aimed at Scott. Scott's agitation led him to believe that Scott thought that Traill had charged him with unfairly firing too soon. The only sentence which was intelligible to Patmore will permit that interpretation if Patmore's mistaken inference is understood: "What! did not Mr. Christie fire at me! [just at the time I fired at him]." Patmore thought Scott's statement was argumentative, not interrogative. He "was fearful, from the irritation of Mr. Scott's words and manner at this time, that he might say something offensive, which would place the probability of an adjustment still farther off: he therefore urged Mr. Scott to be silent." (Patmore's MS Apologia, first published in Champneys, II, 426–29).

However the blame is to be apportioned in this tragedy of errors, the reader should remember three facts in fairness to Patmore. Christie had first requested the meeting at night which made it extremely difficult, if not impossible, for the opposing second to see his noble action of firing to one side. Traill did not speak at all until the pistols were reloaded, and then he did not speak directly to Patmore. And Patmore followed the etiquette of the code duello punctiliously in restraining his principal from continuing to speak to a hostile second.

3. A surgeon of Spring-gardens, Pettigrew observed the duel, "rendered all the assistance in his power," and then "returned to town, in order to procure further surgical assistance, and to give directions that Mr. Scott's apartments, at Mr. Botte's, in York-street, should be prepared for his reception." But Scott could not be moved. (*Bell's Weekly Messenger*, 19 February 1821, p. 56.)

4. *Morning Chronicle*, 5 March 1821, with only slight verbal differences from Reynolds's version.

5. It was not printed in the *Times*.

6. On Saturday, March 3. Christie was at Boulogne-sur-Mer. Sir Walter Scott's actions and advice to Christie and Lockhart can be followed in *The Letters of Sir Walter Scott*, ed. H. J. C. Grierson, 12 vols. (London: Constable, 1932–37), VI, 341–92.

7. To flee to Calais temporarily.

8. Robert Baldwin, senior member of Baldwin, Cradock, and Joy, publisher of the *London Magazine*.

9. Caroline Colnaghi Scott. Four of her letters to Patmore, written after the

duel, are printed in Champneys, II, 411–19. The manuscripts are in the Princeton University Library.

10. Sometime before the duel, presumably earlier on Friday, February 16, when he had determined to visit Christie to issue the challenge, Scott had entrusted to Reynolds two letters to be delivered in case of his death, one to Caroline Scott and the other to her brother, Dominic Paul Colnaghi (1790–1879). After Scott's death on February 27, Reynolds delivered both letters to Dominic Colnaghi, relying on his discretion in choosing the time for delivery to the widow.

11. This letter is not among those printed in Champneys and preserved in the Princeton Library.

12. Many years later Smith wrote an account of the duel, which agrees with the one in this letter, as part of "A Greybeard's Gossip about His Literary Acquaintance," New Monthly Magazine, LXXXI (December 1847), 416–18.

13. The asterisk was added by Patmore. After a corresponding asterisk below Reynolds's signature, Patmore wrote, "See R's letter Mar 23." That letter follows in this book. The passage before the asterisk in the text is marked in the left margin with a single line from "account of your conduct" through "requested him to" and with a double line from "acknowledge" through "letter."

Reynolds's account of the meeting of Smith, Patmore, and Scott is confusing because Reynolds himself was somewhat confused. As early as late November or early December of 1820 (Patmore said about six weeks before 10 January 1821), Scott suspected that his November attack in the London on Blackwood's might cause Lockhart to call him out. He wrote Patmore, asking whether he would serve as second (the letter is published in Derek Patmore, "A Literary Duel," Princeton University Library Chronicle, XVI [Autumn 1954], p. 17). After he had replaced Patmore as second with Smith, he sought to keep everything out in the open by having Smith assure Patmore that he (Smith) had agreed to serve as second even though he knew that he was a second choice. Scott later reverted to Patmore when Smith, unable to effect pacification, refused on principle to take part in a duel.

Patmore undoubtedly marked the passage because he was outraged at Scott's account of his conduct ("too forward and inconsiderate") and he doubly underlined the passage about the letter because he still had the letter to use as evidence that Scott had told what he and Caroline Scott regarded as a white lie to salve Smith's feelings. That Patmore would be unlikely to press Scott into a duel is supported by Caroline Scott's remark in a letter to him that in an earlier quarrel he had succeeded in preventing a duel between Scott and an unspecified opponent (Champneys, II, 414).

14. John Ramsay McCulloch (1789–1864), editor of the Scotsman newspaper and vehement opponent of Blackwood's Magazine. Scott had doubtless seen him on his vacation in Edinburgh in the summer of 1820 (London Magazine, I, 495) and continued to correspond with him about his attacks on Blackwood's. McCulloch probably furnished Scott with much of the information which he used in his articles in the London.

15. A club. Earlier, from 1807 to 1816, George Ragget had operated a gambling house at 21 St. James's Square under the name of the Union Club (George H. Cunningham, London [London: J. M. Dent and Sons, 1927], p. 601).

16. Rice's pen slip for an ampersand.

17. Below the signature, Patmore wrote "legal position."

17

TO PETER G. PATMORE

23 March 1821

ALS: In the Princeton University Library. As with the last letter, Champneys printed a faulty version, II, 422–25.
Address: Mr. Mr. P. G. Pitt/ Post Restante/ Calais. Postmark: F 21 130.

50 Poland Street
23 March 1821

My Dear Patmore

I have a great deal to say to you, and have very little time left to say it in; for I have been engaged all this morning in seeing first Mrs Scott (who by the sensible reasoning of my good friend Mrs Montagu[1] has recognized the propriety of allowing the conversation I requested) then D^r. Darling & then Mrs Scott again. She is perfectly willing and anxious to do you all the justice in her power, and feels very deeply for the distressing & fearful situation in which you are cast. I stated to her the apprehension that I had of a vindictive feeling on the part of the prosecution, & expressed myself anxious to learn the disposition with which the trial would be conducted on the part of her Family. She distinctly & positively assured me that the utmost anxiety existed in the breasts of all parties to proceed with the most lenient feeling. They would do anything, regard being had to the honor & memory of Scott, to shield the involved parties from danger. She is clear in her opinion that Scott did not make the statement, which Dr Darling has given, under the impression that he was a dying man, for she recollects that hope was held out to him both by Darling & Guthrie that he might recover,—and the latter gentleman stated to him that ⟨he had⟩ the wound was not necessarily mortal,—that there was a chance of recovery—that he had known others recover, in the same state.[2] This of course (as far as can be foreseen) will annul Darling's evidence. Mrs Scott had heard what Horace Smith stated, and now assured me that it arose entirely from Scott's wish to ⟨re⟩ render his *second-hand* application to Smith proper and delicate towards the latter. She declares that he was satisfied as to your conduct fully, & was averse to applying to Smith;—but that her fears operated upon him, & at her request only was the application made. I do not see that any evidence she could offer would at all be serviceable to your case, for Scott never spoke to ⟨you⟩ her upon the business except when she applied to him at Elder's request,[3]—or to say that he felt for you. On the night of the Duel he certainly told his wife that there had been mismanagement, & that he ought not to have been in the state she saw him in. She is confident that he had no idea of *your* being in danger—that he thought Christie was, & therefore he expressed himself as he did. We shall ascertain now pretty correctly as to whether Darling's evidence will, or will not be received,[4] and that will guide us as to M^rs. Scott;—though assuredly the cruelty of our producing her would be looked upon with dangerous feelings by a Jury—& that "craves wary walking." She however is ready to do all that is right, & will now see me whenever it is required. She says if *I* instead of Rice had gone she would have seen me before, & even now she will not see him or any stranger.[5] My friend M^rs. Montagu has behaved very kindly to her, & certainly has done us all the good by her representations of the duty Mrs Scott owed to all parties to shield you with the truth. I saw Darling, as I before stated, this morning,—& had a long conversation with him, in which I represented the dangerous effects of his evidence as far as your life even was concerned. He confessed that Scott was not destitute of hope when the statement was made,—& he is not aware of it having been Scott's impression that the words were uttered as words to be used against the parties. I shall see Guthrie to confirm what I hear of *his* evidence.

I have given you this account of my interview with M^rs. Scott before I relate the particulars of the conference I have had with Mr Curwood & Mr Adolphus—(though that took place at Maidstone on Wednesday evening)[6] because I am sure you will be most anxious to know her feelings respecting you. I now proceed to inform you of the opinions of counsel on your case, as far as they can at present give them. They consider it of the highest importance that you should assign over your property before trial, as a verdict of manslaughter would cause a forfeiture;—and we must not deceive ourselves with the expectation of any decision more favourable. Mr Rice is now in the city & will see Mr Mount on the subject. I shall therefore leave it to him to inform you of the best means of effecting this assignment. Mr Curwood will arrange as to your surrender, so that you will only have to appear on the morning of trial—& thus avoid the confinement in Newgate for any previous time. They are very fearful of calling M^rs. Scott as an evidence,—and now that the feeling of the prosecutors is known to be so favourable,—and the evidence of Darling is so question-able I am pretty sure that they will not risk the odium of a measure which ⟨all⟩ at the best would be considered cruel & selfish. They advise a simple, sincere, feeling & humble defence—and this we are immediately about to write for you.—As to your surrender at all They cannot risk advice.[7] It can only be for your own decision. They state that you should be possessed of every danger that awaits your situation & that then you must resolve for yourself. You are quite aware of the possible danger,—and will decide accordingly.

I also today saw Mr Brown the Keeper of Newgate who having seen your Father on the subject & knowing Mr Rice intimately, called to say that what he could do, he would. he will in case of your after confinement do what he can to make it as light as possible—He will see me again & arrange as to the surrender on the Friday morning.[8]

You are aware, I dare say, by the newspapers that a sub-scription has been set on foot by ⟨Mr⟩ several persons for Mrs. Scott's benefit; a measure which I cannot but consider extremely improper at this time, in as much as it may excite the minds of the Public, & therefore of the Jurors still further on the subject. Baldwin has this morning sent me a paragraph for my perusal & approval as a communication in the Lion's Head, of the sub-scription &c. I shall return it with a request that for one month it may be postponed, as the Legal Inquiry will then be concluded, and no ill effects can ensue its publication.[9]

I should have told you that Mrs Scott's feeling is very strong against Christie,—that she considers him to have gained a handsome name, unjustly, in the cause. She regards him with the strongest sentiment of disgust & pain.

It now only remains for me to speak on the subject of your return. For my own part I consider it dangerous,—but Rice thinks that if you were quietly to come over & take a retired lodging near us, and inform *us only* of your residence,—that you might then be in London safely for the remainder of the time before trial. One thing would be in your favour, & that is the belief in every person's mind that you are abroad. If you determine on coming (and certainly on many points your presence would now be highly desirable)—you need not say a word about it till you arrive. You might then take a quiet lodging in your now name

—refer to Mr Rice for character &c—& send us word where we may come to you. But unless you can determine on seeing no one, on not writing to any person, or going out at all,—your retirement would be quite hazardous. To be sure the time is near, should you be discovered; but a confinement would be irksome and expensive at best.—In this you must judge from your own sentiments.— Rice has requested me to leave him room for a few words,—and I shall here therefore close my letter. We send to your Mother at all times.[10]

> I am my Dear Sir
> Yours very faithfully
> J H Reynolds

Rice has this moment returned—and as he expects that you will most likely adopt the course of coming to England, he will not do anything in the assignment until then, or until he hears from you on the subject. [*Two illegible words canceled*] present or absent it is a step that you must take, & if he does not hear by the next post of your intention of returning, he will immediately see Mr Mount & other parties interested on the subject. He has seen your Father,[11] Mother, & Mr Stevens[12] this morning—who send letters to you.

1. Mrs. Basil Montagu (née Benson). Reynolds was closely associated with her and her circle for some time. In December 1820 he was corresponding sentimentally with her (KC, II, 365–66), just as Carlyle did later. His close friend, Bryan Waller Procter, married her daughter by a previous marriage, Anne Skepper, on 7 October 1824.

2. George James Guthrie (1785–1856) was a "celebrated" surgeon, to use Sir Walter Scott's adjective, who attended Scott at Chalk Farm Tavern, along with Robert Bree (Keats's surgeon), Dr. Poynter, Dr. Darling, and Dr. Brooks. Guthrie had served with distinction as an army surgeon from 1801–1814; perhaps he was the more inclined to be optimistic because much of his reputation was based on saving men badly wounded in battle. Guthrie's early optimism was generally circulated: for examples, see *Letters of Sir Walter Scott*, VI, 363, and *Bell's Weekly Messenger*, 19 February 1821, p. 56.

3. On February 20, three days after Scott's statement to Darling but seven days before Darling made the statement public, Patmore was so troubled by a *Times* paragraph suggesting that he and Scott knew Christie had not aimed *before* the second fire that he sent this friend Elder, a stranger to John and Caroline Scott, to Chalk Farm Tavern to get a clear statement of the fact. Caroline wrote it at her husband's dictation, and then read it aloud for his confirmation (Champneys, II, 428). The statement was as follows:

"Mr. Scott was not made aware till *after* his second fire that Mr. Christie had said that he had discharged his pistol in the air, no communication to that effect having been made by Mr. Traill to Mr. Patmore. Such a statement, had it been understood, would have been deemed by Mr. Scott and his friend completely satisfactory, and would necessarily have prevented any further proceedings.

"The proposal to meet at night, Mr. Scott states to have originated with Mr. Christie, but Mr. Scott willingly acceded to it, in order that the affair might be terminated as quickly as possible." (Champneys [I, 13], overlooking the passage in Reynolds's letter, wrote that the friend's name was unknown).

4. Though given at the coroner's inquest, it was not admissible at the trial for the reason Reynolds indicated in his previous discussion. The statement of a man who knew he was dying could be given, because that realization was regarded as having the force of an oath, but the testimony of a man who thought he might recover could not be admitted. This was a crucial point in Patmore's defense, as Reynolds realized.

5. Because of his association with Scott on the *Champion* from 1815 through 1817 and on the *London* after March 1820, Caroline knew Reynolds rather well, but she had not met Rice.

6. March 21. John Adolphus (1768–1845), who entered himself at the Inner Temple and was called to the bar in 1807, specialized in criminal law.

7. Patmore underlined this sentence heavily and marked the rest of the paragraph with two lines in the left margin. Below the underlined sentence, he wrote "£10,000," the value of the estate which he might lose by forfeiture if convicted.

8. It seems to have been the custom to hold trials of this type at the Old Bailey on Fridays. Both trials were held on Friday: that of Christie and Traill on Friday, April 13, and that of Patmore on Friday, June 8.

9. Despite Reynolds's objection to Baldwin, the appeal was printed prominently and at length in the next month's "Lion's Head," *London Magazine*, III (April 1821), 359. There was no delay; the March number had been issued before Scott died.

10. Maria Clarissa Stevens Patmore (1761–1853).

11. Peter Patmore, retired silversmith and jeweler.

12. Robert Stevens (born c. 1760), Patmore's maternal uncle.

18

TO JAMES A. HESSEY

January 1823

Reprinted from *KC*, II, 429.
Address: Mr. Hessey.

Dear Hessey

Certainly tomorrow Morning as soon as you please after 10. I am equally harassed & hardworked just now with yourself.—I shall also send you then a short paper on Mrs Siddons—and say whether the foll^g day will do for T. Moore[1]

Ever truly yrs
J H Reynolds

1. For these articles see the next letter.

19

TO JAMES A. HESSEY

January 1823

Reprinted from *KC*, II, 429–30. The reference to Oakley (none of the twelve Oakleys listed in Pigot's *Commercial Directory*, 1823–24, throws any light on the subject) suggests that this letter was written shortly before Hessey's letter of January 21 and 22 (no. 324 in *KC*, II, 431–32).
Address: Mr Hessey.

Sat^y

Dr Hessey

A friend dropped inopportunely in upon me last night & cut Tom Moore[1] off. I send you *Sarah*.[2] Of course Monday would be too late—If not—I could do the thing well tomorrow—Just say whether or not it would do.

I wrote to Oakley last night to say that you would meet him half way & take £37.10.—at a word—& that considering you were the losers of £8.8.—rent, I thought the offer liberal. He has not answered me. The moment I hear—you shall hear.

Ever yrs
J H Reynolds

Write—do not send *verbally*—as I am no Author in the Bearer's eyes.

1. Moore's *Loves of the Angels* was reviewed in the *London Magazine*, VII (February 1823), 212–15.
2. "Mrs. Siddons's Abridgement of Paradise Lost," *London Magazine*, VII (February 1823), 216. Both Moore and Mrs. Siddons are included by Reynolds in "The Literary Police Office, Bow-Street, No. VIII," *London Magazine*, VII (February 1823), 160.

20

TO JOHN TAYLOR

January 1823(?)

Reprinted from *KC*, II, 430–31. The date is a guess. The letter may have been written after that preceding. Reynolds had long been an unreliable contributor: in the *London Magazine*, October 1822 (VI, 291), the editor mentions "a welcome paper from the *late* Mr. Edward Herbert—why did he not send it sooner." In September, 1823 (VIII, 235), he says: "Edward Herbert's Letter on a Peculiar Race of Men and Horses is come to hand:—we thought he had been dead."

Address: Mr Taylor or Mr Hessey/ Fleet Street.

Monday

Dear Taylor

You must excuse my *failing* you once more—but I am off for Devonshire tomorrow And the many many things I am compelled to do—& have been—before leaving is more than you can imagine. Think of me, my Dear Taylor, as a Friend who will not always thus deceive you—I saw Hood this morning as I was going to Dr Stodart's part of the world but I cannot explain why I am thus faulty. I only know I have fagged myself to death.

I shall be ashamed ever to meet you.

Ever, however, truly
& kindly yours
J H Reynolds

21

TO JOHN TAYLOR

15 August 1823

Reprinted from *KC*, II, 445.
Address: John Taylor Esq/ 13 Waterloo Place.

Great Marlbro Street
15 Augt 1823

My Dr Taylor

The Bearer of this note is the Gentleman of whom I spoke to you yesterday as the Author of a Work upon Latin Verse. I am quite sure you will give his Book every attention—and that you will advise him for the best in furthering ⟨his⟩ its publication. By so doing you will add one other obligation to the many I already am indebted to you for

I am Dr Taylor
Most truly yours
J H Reynolds

22

TO JAMES A. HESSEY

June 1824(?)

Reprinted from *KC*, II, 462–63. The date is a guess. The letter may be a sort of reply to Taylor's of 11 June 1824, *KC*, II, 457–60. On the other hand, it may have been written, say, on Saturday, 22 March 1823, when the "Drama" herein promised was still expected by Hessey in no. 330, *KC*, II, 440–41.

Address: Mr Hessey/ 93 Fleet Street/ JHR.

Sat^y Night

Dear Hessey

This will be delivered to you early on Sunday morning. This Evening I should have sent but owing to my cursed habit of procrastinating the Drama, I have delayed it until every hour is precious. Tomorrow Morning, the moment it is done I shall send it—& I shall be at the desk between 7 & 8. I have been this Evening at a Client's Accounts (the *worst* subject for me) from 8 until after 10—And I am hurt beyond measure at the inconvenience I put you to. I shall write on tomorrow but say what you want—will 4 pages be too much—or will 3 of the Drama & something short do—Tomorrow is heartily at your Service—& mind that the profit of the paper goes to the extra charge of the printer. This I quite insist upon.

Yours ever truly
J H Reynolds

My Servt shall come away the moment I finish.

23

TO JAMES A. HESSEY

About 1825(?)

Reprinted from *KC*, I, 283. The paper is watermarked 1824, but the date of 1825 is a mere guess. Perhaps Reynolds refers to nos. 107 and 77 in *KC*, I, 223–28 and 164–67.

Great Marlbro S^t
Thursday

Dear Hessey

I know not how you came to conclude that I had Severn's letter giving an account of Keats' Death.—The fact is I never even read it or saw it. Taylor lent me one of Severn's letters to Haslam, written on the arrival of himself & Severn—& that letter I have now—But the particular one you want I can give you no account of.

Yours ever
J H Reynolds

24

TO CHARLES W. DILKE

15 February 1831

As quoted in Dilke, *Papers of a Critic*, I, 25.

Brighton, 15th Feb., 1831.

My Dear Dilke,

You astound me with your fall. It is more decided than Milton's "Noon to Dewy Eve" one! From 8d. to 4d. is but a step, but then it is also from the sublime to the ridiculous.[1] Remember what an increase must take place to get it all home. A sale of 6000! Mercy on us! I certainly hoped the change would allow us to lower our outgoings, and consequently fatten our profits. But after the cost of writers, printers, duty, and paper, what in the name of the practical part of a farthing remains to report upon as profit. A midway lowering of price would better suit the public and ourselves. 6d. unstamped! There is something more respectable, too, in the sum. Something less Tattlerish, and Mirrorish and Two-penny-Trashish! However, do what you please. If apoplexy is the fancy, my head is ready, and I am prepared to go off. Consumption, which I take to be a complaint arising out of non-consumption—*lucus a non lucendo*—is a sad death for us very lively critics.

1. Dilke planned to cut the price of the *Athenaeum*, of which he was part-owner and editor. As a result of the disapproval shown in this and the following letter, Reynolds and Hood sold their shares in the magazine, much to their later detriment as Dilke prospered increasingly from his gamble.

25

TO CHARLES W. DILKE

15 February 1831

As quoted in Dilke, *Papers of a Critic*, I, 26, where the date is said to be that of the preceding letter.

Dear Dilke,

Hood and I have been calculating this afternoon, and the result is appalling. To lower below 6d. would, in my opinion, be an unadvisable course, and such a fall would show that our previous state was hopeless. The difference between 6d. and 4d. would be 8*l*. 6s. 8d. a week in a thousand copies. The loss per annum on 5,000 copies would be 2,165*l*. And you should remember that this very 2d. is in reality the cream of the profit, for between the expenses and the 4d. there can be the merest shadow of a gain. We are quite against the total change in our paper-constitution which you threaten.

J. H. R.

26

TO JAMES WINSTON

16 September 1831

Reprinted from *KC*, II, 467–68. Winston (1779–1843) was secretary of the Garrick Club, founded in 1831, and the author of *The Theatric Tourist* (1805). Numerous volumes of theater programs and clippings about the stage compiled by him, as well as several manuscripts he wrote on theatrical subjects, are in the Theater Collection at Harvard. In *The Garrick Club*, p. 42, R. H. Barham (1788–1845), author of *The Ingoldsby Legends*, included this notice of Reynolds: "An old schoolfellow of mine at St. Paul's School; an attorney in Golden Square; author of 'Peter Corcoran,' and many other anonymous works of great merit, especially of a paper on Lady Mary W. Montagu in Bentley's *Miscellany* and sundry papers in the *Athenaeum*."
Address: J. Winston Esq/ 3 Charles Street/ Covent Garden.

27 Golden Square
16 Sept. 1831

D[r] Sir

I shall be happy to have ⟨myself⟩ my name inserted in the list of original Members of the Garrick Club.—And I shall be obliged by your communicating my wish to the Committee.

I am D[r] Sir
Your faithf[l] Serv[t]
J. H. Reynolds

27

TO CHARLES W. DILKE

1830-38

The three undated notes included here were published by Sir Charles W. Dilke in *Papers of a Critic*, I, 27–28, 45. They were written during the period from 1830, when Dilke began editing the *Athenaeum*, to 1838, when Reynolds ceased regular contributing to the *Athenaeum* in order to edit the *New Sporting Magazine*.

[*Along with some verse for the* Athenaeum, *Reynolds wrote:*] I hope, as I write for my bread, you do not *weigh-in poetry as bone.*

[*Another note:*] Dear D., are you mad, or only brazen? How on earth could I read three volumes of dullish chit-chat, and write a paper on it by Wednesday morning? You might as well have sent me the Ency. Brit. to turn into verse in the same time!

[*Returning a book sent him for review:*] That you may consign it to some independent hand, according to your religious custom. I, alas! know both author *and* bookseller!

28

TO THE COMMITTEE OF THE GARRICK CLUB

1833(?)

ALS: In the Garrick Club Papers in the Theater Collection at Harvard. The petition is undated; all who signed were members in 1833, according to a printed membership list in the Garrick Club Papers.

The Committee are earnestly requested to take into consideration the propriety of [*illegible word canceled*] fitting up—a Billiard Table—subject to such regulations as they may deem fit

J H Reynolds

[*Signatures by the various hands*]

B Duruset	George Cates
Henry R Addison	Henry Robertson
R A Price	J. P Collier
James Moyes	William Abbott

W. F. White   R. Ovey
T. N. Talfourd   A E A Dillon
T. De Trueba Cosio   Biggs Andrews
J Terrail   William Reade
{J}[1] Poole   William Barham
{Jam}es Duncan   G. Heathcote L Life Guard
                               William Macready
                               F. S. Murphy

1. The page is torn.

29

TO RICHARD BENTLEY

4 February 1835

ALS: In the University of Illinois Library. The publisher Richard Bentley (1794–1871) had been a schoolmate of Reynolds at St. Paul's School.
Address: Richard Bentley Esq/ New Burlington Street.

27 Golden Square
4 Feb. 1835

Sir

I have seen Mr Poole[1] who is I assure you most deeply annoyed at the Advertizement & 2 paragraphs in todays Chronicle.[2] The whole is, as he states, a complete mis representation of the work he had merely to Edit. Mr Poole desires me to state that he will under these circumstances have nothing to do with the work—calculated as it must be, by such ⟨def⟩ deceptive announcements as have appeared, to injure his reputation and mislead the Public. He will, through me, repay you the £50—[*two illegible words canceled*] on the agreement being cancelled—But if you insist on holding to it—he will send to the newspapers this Evening a letter, a copy of which the Bearer of this will shew you. I should have again seen you on this unpleasant subject, but am unable to leave my House just now

I am Sir
Yr obt Sert
J. H. Reynolds

To R. Bentley Esq

1. John Poole (1786 or '87–1872) was a prolific dramatist and comic writer, best known for *Paul Pry* (1825), whom Reynolds had known at least as early as 1820 when they both contributed to the *London Magazine*.

2. The *Morning Chronicle*, 4 February, 1835, printed an advertisement of a "New Work by the Author of 'Paul Pry' . . . Romances of Many Lands, with Sketches of Life and Manners, Comic and Serious"; a paragraph under "New Publications" listing the work as "By John Poole, Esq."; and a subsequent paragraph congratulating readers on their good fortune in having the work which Poole had "recently been engaged in preparing."

30

TO RICHARD BENTLEY

4 February 1835

ALS: In the University of Illinois Library.
Address: Richard Bentley Esq/ New Burlington/ Street.

27 Golden Square
4 Feb. 1835

Sir

Will you oblige me with a reply to my letter,—as time presses, and I have to act upon Mr Poole's intentions & directions. I have taken no step as you requested until this time—But I shall now have to send to the Newspaper offices[1]

I am Sir Yr ob^t Servt
J. H. Reynolds

To R. Bentley Esq

1. Poole's letter did not appear in the newspapers. Reynolds succeeded in withdrawing his name from *Romances of Many Lands*. On February 6 the *Chronicle* included a paragraph which had been "requested" and which described the book without mentioning Poole's name.

31

TO JAMES WINSTON

12 January 1837

ALS: In the Garrick Club Papers in the Theater Collection at Harvard.

10 Great Marlbro' St.
12 Jan^r 1837

Dear Sir

Allow me to acknowledge the receipt of your letter[1] & through you to thank the Committee of the Garrick Club for the handsome Communication they have made to me. I I[2] assure you it has been most gratifying to me to have had the opportunity of contributing, Even a trifle, to the marks of respect shewn to the last of the Kembles

I have the Honor to be
Dr Sir
Your faith Serv
J. H. Reynolds

To J. Winston Esq

1. See Appendix, p. 73.
2. The second *I* is repeated on the second page.

32

TO P. F. LAPORTE

28 April 1837

ALS: In the Huntington Library. I am grateful to Paul Zall for the information that this note and the later one of 27 May 1837 were originally in a grangerized copy of Moore's *Life of Byron* before they were transferred to the manuscript collection. Both notes were sent by messenger, rather than mailed.
Address: Private/ P. F. Laporte Esq.

Dear Laporte

I now trust that the House of last night will enable you to spare me the £200 tomorrow morning.—[1]I am intitled to ask the fulfilment of your promise—an arrangement known to Mr. Lumley.[2] I put it to you as earnestly as I can.

Yours truly
J H Reynolds

10 Great Marlbro S^t.
28 Apl 1837.

1. Evidently Reynolds had done some work, either legal or theatrical, for P. F. Laporte (died 1841), who was manager of King's Theatre, the leading opera house. On the evening before, "a densely crowded audience" was so enthusiastic about a revival of *Don Giovanni* that repeated performances were assured (*Athenaeum*, 6 May 1837, p. 330). Reynolds believed that Laporte now had the money to pay him.
2. Benjamin Lumley (1811–75), financial manager of King's Theatre.

42

33

TO P. F. LAPORTE

27 May 1837

ALS: In the Huntington Library.
Address: P. F. Laporte Esq.

10 Great Marlbro S^t.
27 May 1837

Dear Laporte

On my return to Town I find your letter & will attend to it.

I was in hopes when I saw your handwriting that you were about to fulfil our arrangement—But you say not a word about it.

If this money cannot be paid to me now it never can. Will you manage it for me to day?—

Yours truly
J H Reynolds

34

TO JOHN TAYLOR

31 October 1837

Reprinted from *KC*, II, 468–69.

10 Great Marlbro S^t
31 Oct. 1837

Dear Taylor

We are now strangers,—We, who were " in the better part of your life, & the happiest part of mine" always together,— never now meet. There is a wish amongst a few of my private friends that some of my papers should be housed into volumes— and I who have walked through life with a skeleton of reputation without a particle of name, enter into this wish. You remember how sadly though how rapidly my work went off!—Five "sub-scribed" the Edition, though Longmans would not take a copy.[1] What can be done as to permission? Tell me. You have the right in the London Mag^e papers—is it not so?—I know—or think I know—that the style of publication is quite out of your way—but if it be so—I do not think you will withold from me the chance of

43

whispering my very important secret to the public. I give you my word at this moment I have not a Publisher in my eye—But one may, with your leave, occur.—

What days—were *the* days of the London!—I "try back"[2] as the Huntsman says—over the hours of Early-Hood—Earnest-Hessey—bleak Dr Darling—twinkling Clare,—"tipsy-joy & jollity"-Lamb—Drear-Carey,—Long-*taled* Cunningham—and beautiful Mrs Jones![3]—Where are all?—or most of them?—

I am always dabbling with my pen—like a grey-headed Duckling—old in myself—but young in my love of the stream. You are always publishing good books—which are quite out of my line

Yours truly
J H Reynolds

—I *do* believe I am asking you for nothing—and it is the thing usually conceded to requests asking more.

1. Of Reynolds's "Edward Herbert" articles in the *London Magazine*, Marsh says in *J. H. R.: Poetry and Prose*, p. 28: "Advertisements indicate a plan to publish them in book form 'with etchings by George Cruikshank.' The book seems never to have been issued . . . ." Two of Cruikshank's etchings for it are still in existence: see A. M. Cohn's *George Cruikshank* (London: Bookman's Journal, 1924), p. 271.
2. *NED* defines as "to go back . . . so as to cover ground afresh where something has previously been missed" and dates its first example 1816.
3. Mrs. Isabella Jones. See Gittings, *John Keats*, pp. 139–40 and passim.

35

TO JAMES WINSTON

1837(?)

ALS: In the Garrick Club Papers in the Theater Collection at Harvard. Undated. The conjectural 1837 is offered because in Reynolds's preceding two letters of 1837 he wrote from the same address, 10 Great Marlborough Street. In the 1820s his address had been 27 Great Marlborough Street, but in later years he recorded different addresses except for 1837.
Address: Mr Winston/ Garrick Club/ King Street/ Covent Garden.

My Dear Sir

Will you oblige me by letting my Servant have 4 very nice mutton chops,—from the excellent meat supplied by the Butcher

44

of the Club. Mrs Reynolds is unwell & is advised to take such food & I am anxious to have it of the best.

Yours faithf.

J. H Reynolds

I shall be at the Club today or tomorrow & can pay the Servant.[1]

Wednesday
10 Grt Marlbro St

1. The postscript was added at the top of the letter.

36

TO CHARLES W. DILKE

18 January 1838

Published in the *Athenaeum*, 20 January 1838, p. 52.

To the Editor of the Athenaeum.

Dear Sir,—

Will you allow me to correct an error about a trifle. In the theatrical criticism in your last week's paper,[1] a little piece at the Haymarket theatre, entitled, "Confounded Foreigners"[2]—which has been received by the public with unusual kindness—is stated to be the joint production of Mr. G. Dance and myself; and that the authors had not had full justice done them in the delivery of the dialogue, &c. Mr. Dance suggested to me the idea of the subject of the piece—a fact which I have acknowledged; and as his view of the way in which it should have been executed wholly differed from mine, it is but right I should say, that, for the construction of the plot, and the entire dialogue, I am solely responsible. I should not trouble you on so pigmy a matter, but that having submitted to the character of being the author of the piece, and certainly most of those who know me being readers of your paper, I am desirous of being understood not to have allowed that to be called mine, which did not belong to me.

I am, dear Sir,
Your faithful servant,

Garrick Club, Jan. 18.   J. H. Reynolds

1. 13 January 1838, p. 36.
2. *Confounded Foreigners: A Farce in One Act*, Vol. III of *The Acting National Drama*, ed. Benjamin Webster (London, n.d.). The play was first performed at the Haymarket on 6 January 1838.

37

TO WALTER SPIERS

February 1839

Based on a typescript owned by J. M. Cohen. Printed in Morgan, "John Hamilton Reynolds and Thomas Hood," p. 92. Spiers was the printer of the *New Sporting Magazine*, which Reynolds edited from 1838 through 1840.

Sunday Night

Dear Sir,

I send you *all—but Turfiana*[1]—I wish you would let all be calculated—so that I may temper the length of *T*. to the space remaining. I am tired to death.

You will find the list now as the annexed list on the other side tells you[2]—& the *star* shews that the M.S. is now with you. I think the Varieties & Notes of the Month[3] may exceed what I have reckoned. Let me hear from you at the Office[4] as soon as possible

Yours truly

J. H. Reynolds

P.S. Get the correspondence in one page by small type.

1. A series of unsigned articles written by Reynolds. He had written the first in 1834, and he contributed four more after he became editor.
2. The list, which is preserved in Mr. Cohen's typescript, consists of the table of contents of *New Sporting* for March.
3. "Varieties" was a regular department, apparently prepared by Reynolds and consisting of extracts from new books with sparse critical comment.
4. 4 Adam Street, Adelphi.

38

TO RICHARD BENTLEY

20 March 1839

ALS: In the University of Illinois Library.
Address: Richd Bentley Esq/ New Burlington Street.

4 Adam Street
Adelphi
20 March 1839

Dear Sir

Our friend Barham[1] spoke to me respecting your Magazine —And I told him I would see you. I was not so fortunate as to meet with you when I called. He stated that you would pay me the best terms—and I should be glad—if you would tell me what those terms are, and whether I am in time for the next N°. with a prose paper of 8 or 10 pages. The title is "Some passages in the lives of wooden legs"[2]—And I have four illustrations by my friend M[r] Thackeray—which I think might be given as wood-cuts.[3] I inclose them,—but pray return them by Bearer,—or send them back to me at your first convenience should you be out. The papers would be four in N°.—& one cut for each.[4]

Yours truly

J. H Reynolds

I wrote to Barham, on the subject,—but as Time runs, & *his* time may be better passed,—I think it well to write to you.

When you can put your hand on my paper on the Winds,— which I find is thought *flat*-ulent,—will you cover it up & return it to me.

1. Barham and Reynolds had been Bentley's schoolmates at St. Paul's.
2. It was printed with an altered title, "Some Passages in the Literary Life of Olinthus Jenkinson, Barrister-at-Law," *Bentley's Miscellany*, V (June 1839), 627–32. If not simply nonsense to set the tone for a comic article, the "wooden legs" may originally have been a metaphor for the lifeless rejected manuscripts which "Jenkinson" reported accumulating.
3. The illustrations by Thackeray were not printed, but Reynolds's burlesque summaries of the naval novel, the fashionable novel, and the sentimental novel furnished likely subjects for caricature.
4. Reynolds carried out his plan, contributing three more Jenkinson articles to complete the series of four: "Some Passages in the Literary Life of Olinthus Jenkinson, Adventures of a Maintop-Crosstree-Man," *Bentley's Miscellany*, VI (July 1839), 73–78; "The Harem Unveiled," VI (October 1839), 389–95; and "The Round Table," VII (February 1840), 194–202.

39

TO RICHARD H. BARHAM

3 April 1839

ALS: In the Houghton Library at Harvard, H C L. ENG. 936. II, 69.

4 Adam Street

Adelphi

3[d] Apl 1839

My Dear Sir

I want to have a few minutes conversation with you— ⟨which⟩ respecting a M. S. which I ⟨want⟩ have a notion of

47

publishing—and of which I want the Authorship to be strictly a secret.

Truly yours

J H Reynolds

Shall you be at the Club[1] to day—or when can I call on you?

1. The Garrick Club at 35 King Street, where Reynolds met congenially with Barham and Thackeray. An undated note of Thackeray's reveals the close association of the three at the club: "Smoking-Room/ Dear Barham. Reynolds has just raised a wonderful objection to an important article, (of a few lines) wh I have submitted to him. Would you be goodnatured and hear the passage read?/ W M T/ It must be in *secret*" (*The Letters and Private Papers of William Makepeace Thackeray*, ed. Gordon N. Ray, 4 vols. [Cambridge, Mass.: Harvard University Press, 1946], IV, 307).

40

TO JAMES WINSTON

7 December 1839

ALS: In the Garrick Club Papers in the Theater Collection at Harvard.

Garrick Club

7[1] Dec. 1839

Dr Sir

It appears to be the general wish of those Gentlemen of the Club, who smoke,—that the Committee should, if they consistently can with reference to the arrangements of the Club,—appropriate One of the two rooms over the Drawing Rooms for [*two illegible words canceled*] a smoking room. I write this Letter at the request of Mr Power,[2] who states the general wish to be such as I referred to in the opening of this Communication. You will oblige the gentlemen interested in the matter, therefore, by bringing this subject before the Committee

I am Dr Sir

Your faithful Serv

J. H Reynolds

To J. Winston Esq

1. A raised 1 followed by a period after the 7 is probably a pen slip.
2. Tyrone Power, Esq., according to the 1833 membership list in the Garrick Club Papers.

41

TO THOMAS HOOD

13 March 1840

ALS: In the Bristol Central Library. First printed in the *Bookman*, LXIV (September 1923), 277–78. Hood's address at the time, which Reynolds forgot or mislaid, was La Rhetorique, Rue St. Francois (from Jane Hood's ms letter to Dr. Elliot of 4 March 1840 in the Yale Library). He took quite a chance for the sake of his joke in addressing this pleasant letter to "Rue de Something."
Address: Thos Hood Esq/ Rue de *Something*/ Ostend. *Postmarks*: London/ 13 Mar 1840; Paid/ 13 Mar 1840; T P/ Holburn; Angleterre Ostend/ 14 Mars 1840.

13 John Street
Adelphi
13 March 1840

My Dear Hood

Many thanks for the sardines which are delicacies indeed; —they seem to be a sort of anchovy becharmed!—I presented some to my friend Mills, who prized them vastly.[1]

I will arrange with Mr Speirs about the magazines,[2]—and pray let me have the promised paper at your earliest convenience —as the month is careering on again to its close.[3] I do seriously believe that the months are very unlike cherubs, and consist *only* of *Latter Ends*. I am no sooner out of the frying pan of one magazine,—but I am into the fire of the one immediately following. I have been endeavouring once more to get into Westmoreland for 3 or 4 days on pressing business,—but that cursed *thing* which is proverbially said to make a "mare to go" makes me stay, to my great detriment in interest as well as pleasure. I am now,—or rather my new Residence is—undergoing repair & whitewashing: —I wish I could undergo ⟨the⟩ repair myself; *whitewashing*[4] I have gone through.

I hope your health is good enough to allow you to set heartily to work at some new matter,[5] for depend on it, my Dear Hood, this world is all oil to monied gentlemen,—but cayenned-hell-vinegar to pauperized people!—You and I are decidedly very ingenious persons of wit about Town;—but we grow our Talent in so rich a compost of indolence and negligence,—that we hardly produce even *Annuals*.[6] Both of us might have rolled in our own *Dickenses*,—or kept a one Horse *Ainsworth*; but we allow your industrious crawlers and empty Hard-workers to go a-head without a head;—whilst we are limping along with down-at-heel shoes—& hats with the lids off. You could, with your power name, with little trouble make £500 a year out of the magazines only:—But as Roderick Random says "Let me not profane the chaste mysteries of Hymen!"—[7]

Writing from England, I ought to give you some news of your natural Home;—but what would you care to hear about the rise & fall of Theatres—the babble about Prince Albert & the young Lady in gingerbread; the Literary Announcements of Colburn & Bentley;—the laying down of wooden pavements—the taking up of the weather. You are so removed—& have been removed so long; that your sympathies with matters here are below Zero. Then I know nothing of bonnetless heads,—large shrimps,—cheap markets foundered English,—sloppy dishes, &c &c—in all which of course your heart abideth.—Our intercourse therefore (⟨Like⟩ See Commissioner Lin's Chinese manifesto) is "prohibited, *for ever!*"[8]—Were it not for our late short treaty, we should scarcely have one common conversational chair between us to sit down upon.—I must however whisper to you a decent reply I could not *help* making the other day to Eliza—after she had had an explanatory chat with Mrs Dilke about my alleged "speaking against the Athenaeum."—The latter had observed that it was like attempting "to take away their bread"—and Eliza said to me *en passant* "and why should you attempt to take away their bread."—My answer was "because it is *so dry.*"—How poor a consumptive thing is a little joke when you bleed it in ink!

Give my love to Jane, I thank her for her few lines on your sheet of paper—I hope her face—jaw teeth—ear & all the other appurtenances whatsoever have, like mine, taken a whole holiday from pain.[9] I have nothing now but the influenza,—with a ⟨pain⟩ gnaw in my liver through to my shoulderblade,—and a tendency on the part of the whole army of "Innards" to shew inflammatory signs. So that I may say I enjoy the usual portion of good health conceded to mortals.

I should not of course know Fanny,[10] who must by this time have run up into that sort of monument height, such as to make you, as a Parent, keep anxiously watching that in some wayward moment she does [not] come Miss Moyes over you, & throw herself off the top of herself. Tom,[11] I should much have liked to see more of. He is a fine, frank, easy, happy Lad,—and made me quite proud of being an ⟨Aunt⟩ an Uncle.

Eliza does not know I am writing,—or would join me in all regards & good wishes to all.

Yours ever truly

J. H Reynolds

Pray let me hear from you soon.

1. John Mills (died c. 1885), a sporting writer who contributed to *Bentley's Miscellany*. In *A Critical Dictionary of English Literature and British and American Authors*, 3 vols. (Philadelphia, 1888), II, 1289, Samuel A. Allibone lists sixteen books by Mills published from 1838 through 1871, many of them about sporting. The Dedication to *Old English Gentleman* places his home at Brandeston Hall in September 1841.

2. Walter Spiers, 399 Oxford Street, printer of the *New Sporting Magazine*. Having contributed several pieces to the magazine, Hood wanted copies. Earlier he had been somewhat irritated at not receiving them.

3. Reynolds received it in time, "Fishing in Germany," *New Sporting Magazine*, XVIII (April 1840), 253–60.

4. Slang for going bankrupt. The certificate of bankruptcy was issued on 26 October 1838.

5. Reynolds had cause for concern. Hood was gravely ill, as his and Jane's MS letter to Dr. Elliot of 4 March 1840 shows (Yale Library).

6. To ruin the pun by explaining it, Hood's *Comic Annuals*, with which Reynolds assisted.

7. Chapter LXVIII.

8. Lin Tse-su, appointed high commissioner at Canton in 1838, precipitated the Opium War in 1839 by seizing and destroying British opium and by seeking to dictate to the British.

9. Reynolds had seen the Hoods several weeks earlier when they had been in England for a few weeks. Jane had suffered various pains for some time, though by March 4, she was better except for "a pain in my face" (Jane's MS letter to Dr. Elliot in the Yale Library).

10. Frances Freeling Hood, later Mrs. John S. Broderip (1830–78), just ten at the time.

11. Tom Hood (1835–74), five years old.

42

TO THE SOLICITOR FOR ALFRED H. BAILY

19 May 1840

This letter was copied into Hood's bill of complaint against Alfred H. Baily, filed on 22 May 1843 and now at the Public Record Office in London. First printed in Morgan, "John Hamilton Reynolds and Thomas Hood," pp. 93–94.

Your letter requiring me to attend you after two or three days notice . . . has just reached me . . . . I consider that the earliest explanation of what are asserted to be erroneous accounts should have been afforded me here I cannot ask to open a settled account nor do I but I apprehend you are mistaken as to their being one I can and do however require to have a correct account rendered to Mr Hood if the statements at present in my hands are not such as Messieurs Baily & C° intend to abide by your extract from Mr Hoods of the 18th of February refers only to errors discovered on such a perusal of the accounts as the "time permitted" and does not therefore even infer a satisfaction which your quotation would seem to intimate[1]—If I were to answer you by extracts from letters I think Messrs Baily & C° would regret that such a mode of dealing with their accounts was resorted to—My course will be very straight forward with your Clients if I am not immediately satisfied as to the statements made to me and I will venture to say that more extraordinary accounts were never issued from a publishing house I shall commence proceedings against Messrs Baily & C° for the considerable balance due to Mr Hood and I presume you will appear to process for Messrs Baily & C°, tomorrow morning at noon I shall require to have the stock delivered up and such as they withhold I shall also take the proper measures to obtain

1. Hood had long had doubts about whether his publisher, A. H. Baily, was dealing fairly with him. After having lived abroad to reduce expenses since 1835, he returned to London in February 1840 to investigate Baily's accounts (joint MS letter from Jane and Hood to Dr. William Elliot in the Yale Library). Somewhat mollified by his hasty inspection, he wrote the letter to Baily of February 18 which Baily's solicitor sought to use as evidence that Hood had been satisfied that the accounts were in order. Since he believed the accounts not in order, Reynolds would accept no such excuse.

43

TO RICHARD BENTLEY

15 August 1840

ALS: In the University of Illinois Library.
Address: R. Bentley Eq.

My Dear Sir

I send you proof of my industry in the shape of a goodly M. S. for your next Miscellany—for which I am of course in good time. I fear you cannot print it all at once—but I wish for the sake

of its effect, you would. It is a tale in the style of Mad^e. D Aurmont;
—& I think may be liked. To break it, will be to ruin a *thing of fretwork*—However I know it will run 22 or 23 pages of your Mag^e.

Should you break off stop where I have marked at p 28 of the M. S.

I should like to see a Proof.

I have given an Introduct^n, keeping up the Ingoldsby reality.[1]

Yours ever
J. H Reynolds

10 Adam S^t.
Adelphi
15 Augt. 1840
R. Bentley Esq

1. Bentley rejected the tale: nothing resembling either the style or length appeared in the *Miscellany*. It may be the twenty-two-page tale which Reynolds published four years later: "Oriana and Vesperella; or, The City of Pearls," *Ainsworth's Magazine*, V (January, February, March, and April 1844), 130–35, 242–47, 357–61, and 432–36. If so, the "Introduction keeping up the Ingoldsby reality" was excised.

44

TO RICHARD BENTLEY

6 December 1840

ALS: In the University of Illinois Library.

10 Adam Street Adelphi
Sunday Ev^g.
6 Dec.

Dear Sir

I shall have a light paper for you for your next month's Maga of 10 or 12 pages. Tell me your latest day. The title is

The Experiences of the BIVOUACS:
Being the correspondence of an unsettled Family.
LODGING HOUSES AND THEIR KEEPERS.

It may turn out not a bad subject for other papers descriptive of London Scenes Places & Persons,—not yet touched upon—& with a reference to a Volume—But of this we shall see.[1]

Yours truly

J. H Reynolds

R Bentley Esqr

Let me hear at once, for I am laid up to my room for a few days, & shall not be an idle as well as an ill man

1. No article with this title or fitting this description was published in *Bentley's Miscellany*; evidently it was rejected. But a paper published three months later seems to follow roughly from the initial idea: "Messrs. Leach, Battye, and Slug's Managing Chancery Clerk," *Bentley's Miscellany*, IX (March 1841), 293–301. It is not epistolary, as the first evidently was, but it describes an unusual section with comically strange persons, and it places considerable stress on lodging houses. It is signed "H. R.," for Hamilton Reynolds, a signature which he used for other work during his last twelve years.

45

TO THE SOLICITOR FOR ALFRED H. BAILY

26 March 1841

Copied into Hood's bill of complaint against Alfred H. Baily, filed on 22 May 1843 and now at the Public Record Office in London. First printed in Morgan, "John Hamilton Reynolds and Thomas Hood," p. 94.

It is strange that Messrs Alfred Head Baily & Co can give no account of the quantity of stock attached by Mr Follett on or about the day on which the writs were issued against the former at the suit of Mr Hood and respecting which attachment Messrs Alfred Head Baily & Co the Agents of Mr Hood gave no intimation or information to him however an explanation of the facts can be obtained—The request I addressed to you to be allowed to examine the account was made in consequence of the report given by Dr Elliot of Stratford[1] of a conversation had between himself and Mr Baily in which the latter said that he had never known that his accounts were questioned and that his books were always open to inspection—These accounts are so full of errors that I should presume Messrs Alfred Head Baily & Co would be at once ready to see them right but your letter forbids this presumption—I have again therefore to ask you whether Messrs Alfred Head Baily &

54

C° will permit a proper enquiry into the accounts and an adjustment of them.[2]

1. Dr. William Elliot, Hood's physician, close friend, and correspondent.
2. The case against Baily dragged on and was finally won after Hood's death (Walter Jerrold, *Thomas Hood: His Life and Times* [London: Alston Rivers, 1907], pp. 340–41). But Reynolds furnished little further legal assistance, since in June 1841 St. P. B. Hook replaced him as Hood's attorney (Morgan, "John Hamilton Reynolds and Thomas Hood," p. 94). Why Hood replaced Reynolds remains a mystery.

46

TO ROBERT S. MACKENZIE

21 September 1844

ALS: In the collection of the Historical Society of Pennsylvania in Philadelphia. First printed in *Keats-Shelley Journal*, VI (Winter 1957), 101. Robert Shelton Mackenzie (1809–80) contributed to numerous English and Irish newspapers and magazines and published dozens of miscellaneous books.

10 Adam St
Adelphi
21 Sept 1844

Sir

Your friend W. Barrett[1] has my permission to set the words of this Song;[2]—and I enclose you a correct copy. I shall trust to receive the music when published.

I am Sir
Your obt Serv.
J. H. Reynolds

R. S. Mackenzie Esqr

1. Probably Reynolds's error for John Barnett (1802–90), who composed music for hundreds of poems.
2. "Think of Me," Reynolds's best-known lyric from *The Garden of Florence* (London, 1821). A copy agreeing exactly with the published text was appended to this note.

47

TO THOMAS N. TALFOURD

May 1845

Printed from Robert S. Newdick's "Studies in the Literary Works of Sir Thomas Noon Talfourd" (Ph.D. diss., Harvard, 1930). In 1930 it was in the collection of Major S. Butterworth, who resided at Wood End, Queen's Crescent, Southsea, England. Talfourd (1795–1854), best known for his tragedy *Ion* (1836), had praised Reynolds's early poetry and the *Lamia* volume of Keats (whom he knew only through Reynolds) in the *Retrospective Review*, II (1820), 185–206.

10 Adams Street Adelphi
May 1845

My dear Friend.—

I think you will allow me thus to address you, when I say I thank you for your Book.[1] I liked it, & took the liberty of asking you to give to [sic]; and will thank Mrs Talfourd for permitting my request to be allowed.

Let me take this opportunity of recalling pleasurable—no— *happy* events. That I dined with you when you were called to the Bar,[2] that you and I were married on the *same day* & *year*,[3] and that we have "nothing to regret or forgive."

Yours ever truly
J. H. Reynolds

Mr Serjeant Talfourd.

1. *Vacation Rambles and Thoughts*, 2 vols. (London, 1845).
2. 10 February 1821.
3. 31 August 1822.

48

TO EDWARD MOXON

27 November 1846

Reprinted from KC, II, 162. Printed by Marsh, *J. H. R.: Poetry and Prose*, p. 37.

88 Guilford[1] Street
Russell Square
27 Nov 1846

Dr Sir

I have, for the first time, heard from my friend Mr Taylor, this morning—that he has submitted Letters written by Keats to myself (in the confidence of easy correspondence between us)— to Mr M. Milnes for publication. I feel that *I* ought to have been consulted on the subject—and Mr Taylor agrees with me on this point. ⟨An⟩ I must therefore request you[2] will not use any of my letters until you satisfy me that they ought to be made public, & with my consent.

I am Dr Sir

Your ob^t Ser^t

J. H Reynolds

—Moxon Esq

1. Apparently written "Guidford." Reynolds was uncertain how to spell it (see letters of 22 December 1846 and 30 December 1846).
2. Marsh: that you.

49

TO EDWARD MOXON

15 December 1846

Reprinted from *KC*, II, 166–67. Printed by Marsh, *J. H. R.: Poetry and Prose*, pp. 37–38.

88 Guildford Street

15 Decr 1846

Dear Sir

I have been unable to reply to your letter, until the present time.[1]

You state, & of course correctly, that in September 1845 you purchased of Mr Taylor ⟨a Conjoint⟩ "an equal right with himself to publish all or any of the Manuscript Letters and Copies of Letters written by Keats and now in the custody or power of Mr Taylor."—The Copies of ⟨my⟩ the letters addressed by Keats to me, & of the Poems contained in them—were unauthorizedly made by a Mr Woodhouse, to whom I lent them in confidence for perusal only.[2] These Copies came upon the death of Mr Woodhouse into the hands of Mr Taylor;—but you will be aware that He has no power to sell, nor you to purchase, them ⟨right to us⟩ for publication without my privity & consent.

I beg therefore to state (and you will take this as notice) that I object to the use or publication of the letters written by Keats to myself ⟨as⟩ or of the several poems inserted in or accompanying them.

I have it in intention to write my own recollections of

57

Keats,—and I think it will not be considered unreasonable—that
I should avail myself of what I possess & so deeply value.

I am Dear Sir

Yours truly

J. H Reynolds

Edwd Moxon Esq

1. This letter, like the preceding one and no. 52, is written on black-edged
paper, since Jane Reynolds Hood had recently died (4 December 1846).
2. Woodhouse's various transcripts are described at length by Claude L.
Finney, *The Evolution of Keats's Poetry*, 2 vols. (Cambridge, Mass.: Harvard
University Press, 1936), II, 745–62.

50

TO RICHARD M. MILNES

22 December 1846

Reprinted from *KC*, II, 172–74. Printed by Marsh, *J. H. R.: Poetry and Prose*,
pp. 38–39.

R. Monckton Milnes Esq

88 Guilford Street

22 Decr 1846

Sir

I will shortly state my reasons for acting as I have done.[1]
On the 29th of March last I called on Mr Taylor, & spoke to him
on the subject of writing my "Recollections of Keats"—and of
supporting them by his letters & poems. He leant to the intention.
Dr Darling (the mutual friend of Mr Taylor & myself) saw me, &
stated that ⟨he⟩ Mr Taylor only apprehended I should require
too great a remuneration—when I actually used your words—that
it would be "a labour of love,"[2] with me—& that money would
not raise a difficulty. I ⟨hear⟩ then for the first time saw a bound
MS. Book—with all my letters & Poems copied by Mr Woodhouse:—and expressed my annoyance. I recently called on M^r
Taylor, & in the course of conversation, for the first time learned
that he had sold all my copies to Mr Moxon for £50—!—I was
never consulted on the subject,—never considered;—and he had
no more right to receive a farthing—than he had to abuse a
violated confidence. I protested to him—& received a plausible &
offensive letter stating that he had seen Mr Moxon who had

58

promised him that none of my letters should be printed—&
"that my name should not be mentioned in the Memoir!"
Mᵣ Moxon assured me he had said nothing to this effect. I was sure
of this,—& gathered the malice out of the nettle bed.³ It would be
playing Hamlet, without Laertes!—I may merely add, that I lent
all my papers to Mᵣ Woodhouse *for his perusal*—& his perusal
only;—for he was a good & enthusiastic friend of Keats. *He*
meant nothing cringing towards money. Mᵣ Taylor has asked me
to drop the subject—& to pay me over a part of his wretched gain.
If I *do* receive anything—it shall be handed to *you*—for the use of
the family of George Keats.

And now, Sir, I want little "reconsideration of my
decision." All the papers I possess—all the information I can
render—whatever I can do to aid your kind & judiciously intended
work—are at your service!

But a word or two on the great subject of our correspondence. He was hunted in his youth,—before he had strength to
escape his ban-dogs!⁴ He had the greatest power of poetry in him,
of any one since Shakespere!—He was the sincerest Friend,—the
most loveable associate,—the deepest Listener to the griefs &
disappointments of all around him,—"that ever lived in the⁵
tide of times."⁶ Your expressed intentions as to the Life are so
clear & good;—that I seem to have the weight of an undone work
taken from me.

Perhaps when you come to Town I may see you;—but all
my papers, I *distinctly say*, are at your service

I am Sir your faithf¹ Servᵗ—
J. H Reynolds

P. S.

I beg to thank you for your straightforward letter;—It was
all that was required to satisfy my mind as to the surrender of my
letters to any one, for the world's use. Your own honest love of
literature (for I have since the receipt of your letter reassured my
feeling by a reperusal of your three Volumes) will lead you to
forgive me the fair, though troublesome zeal I have shewn towards Keats.

1. On 19 December 1846, Moxon had advised Milnes to write to Reynolds;
see *KC*, II, 167.
2. Thessalonians 1:3. Milnes describes his work thus in the dedication to
Lord Jeffrey in *Life, Letters, and Literary Remains, of John Keats*, 2 vols. (London,
1848), I, vi.

3. Cf. I *Henry IV*, II.iii.10: "Out of this nettle, danger, we pluck this flower, safety."

4. Marsh: bandages.

5. Apparently "them."

6. *Julius Caesar*, III.i.257.

51

TO RICHARD M. MILNES

30 December 1846

Reprinted from *KC*, II, 177–78. Printed by Marsh, *J. H. R.: Poetry and Prose*, pp. 39–40.

88 Guildford Street
Decr 30th

My Dear Sir

I shall have great pleasure in seeing you when you come to Town.

I know nothing of interest in the Hammond[1] days of Keats. The latter never referred to them, except to express his regret that he had undergone "a one of them."

My intimacy with Keats commenced I believe at the close of 1816 or early in 1817. I met him at Leigh Hunt's Cottage in the Vale of Health.[2] He then lived in the Poultry and I could, I am sure (but this I will test by the time I see you) point out the very House.

I find I have a bundle of papers—being orders & decrees &c in a Chancery Suit—They refer to the property left by Mrs Jenning[s], the Grandmother—but except shewing the date of the death of Mrs Rawlings (the Mother of Keats) Feby 1810[3]—and the month & year of the birth of the Poet Oct 1795 I see nothing to be of use to you. However you shall see them. He became of age about the time I first saw him. And he could hardly ⟨hardly⟩ have fulfilled his allotted time with Hammond. Rice knew Keats through me—(as did Dilke & C. Brown)—and was a *very* kind friend of mine. He was in the Law—drew me into that dreary profession—and ultimately took me into partnership. He was a quiet true wit—extremely well read—had great taste & a sound judgment. For every quality that marks the sensible Companion— the valuable Friend—the Gentleman and the Man—I have known no one to surpass him.

Mr Hessey was the Partner of Mr Taylor—& attended to the retail business in Fleet Street. A very respectable person—but of no moment in the memoirs.[4]

You shall see the M.S of Endymion—I had little to do in revising. I can explain to you the Teignmouth letters[5]—Keats wrote a strange and rash preface—and I prevailed on him to cancel it—& place the inscription the book now bears. I have a proof of the cancelled preface[6] somewhere,—but it has escaped into some place I have not yet discovered.

I have answered all your queries to the best of my power. I do not know whether a letter addressed to you with my personal recollections from our first acquaintance, to his leaving England— will be of use—but when I see you & know what you possess— We shall see.

> I am Dear Sir
> Yours faithf^y
> J. H Reynolds

R. Monckton Milnes Esq
   M. P.

1. Keats was apprenticed to the surgeon Thomas Hammond, 1811–15.
2. It was in October 1816; see *KC*, I, 4–5n.
3. She was buried on March 20 (Willard B. Pope, *TLS*, 22 December 1932, p. 977).
4. *KC* proves that he *was* of moment.
5. See Milnes, *Life, Letters, and Literary Remains, of John Keats*, I, 120–30, and *Letters*, I, 266–83, for the letters Keats wrote from Teignmouth.
6. See letter 56, note 3, below, for an account of the canceled preface which Milnes eventually printed long after Reynolds's death.

52

TO THE COMMITTEE OF THE GARRICK CLUB

21 January 1847

ALS: In the Garrick Club Papers in the Theater Collection at Harvard.

> 80 Guilford Street
> Russell Square
> 21 Jan^r 1847

Gentlemen

    I am not in the habit of appearing before you either on the back of a Bill or the face of a Complaint. I have now to make a request to which I think every Member of the Committee will at once cheerfully accede.

The Porter in the Hall, is not a remarkably strong Man in head or health. He is exposed to a severe season without any of the accomodations allowed at other Clubs to Persons in his situation. I would ask that a Hall chair be [*word illegible*] ordered for him & a rug allowed to separate his feet from the Oilcloth.[1]

> I am Gent
> Your Faithf Serv
> J. H Reynolds

To the Committee of the Garrick Club.

1. Reynolds's kindness toward the old porter seems the more commendable when set against demands by several other members that he be discharged for senility (Garrick Club Papers).

53

TO RICHARD M. MILNES

2 July 1847

Reprinted from *KC*, II, 226–28. This letter minus its two postscripts is printed by Marsh, *J. H. R.: Poetry and Prose*, pp. 40–41.

> Newport
> Isle of Wight
> 2ᵈ July 1847

My Dear Sir

Partly illness—partly the arrangements attend^ت on the setting a new Measure into action here; but chiefly ⟨from⟩ a most earnest desire to find the proof of the original preface to Endymion (which from the confusion of all things in my transfer of them here ⟨is⟩ perplexes me as to its whereabouts) have delayed my reply to your Letter. I am as yet baffled in my search—but I know I have it somewhere.[1]

I regret that your own cause for sorrow[2] and *any* cause on my part should delay the work most interesting to all Lovers of a real Poet. Let me hope that you will find now, in the weaving together of your magic web, ⟨find⟩ a solace—which no other labour can so truly bring you!

I send you some—Documents which may be of use. The copy of the Chancery Proceeding will shew you that Keats was

62

born in Octr 1795—it also shews the date of the death of his
Mother. You may rely on these dates, as they were verified to
support the order. I send you also the Administrations &c in my
possession.

I also place in your hands the original M.S. of 3 of the
Canto's of Endymion. These are further interesting as shewing
the places at which they were finished and when. With this
precious (to me) M.S. I ⟨add⟩ inclose the *original* M.S.S. of the
Ode to the Nightingale, & to Psyche.

In my letters—I have a few unpublished Poems—but these
of course you have.

I shall be glad to hear immediately that you receive my
packet safely; and I am sure I need not say that when you have
done with the contents, you will keep them till I receive them at
your hands.

Is there anything more I can do, to help you in your good
work for my ever valued friend. I am My Dear Sir

Yours truly

J. H Reynolds

R. M. Milnes Esq

P.S.

I add ⟨the⟩ a few small Poems, lest you should not have
seen them. The lines

"Think not of it Sweet One"
&c"

you will find in the *rough* Dra^t at the last page of the Book that
contains the 3 last Cantos of Endymion.

The beautiful story of "Isabella" from Boccacio already
printed—was written with the intention of producing ⟨it⟩ in
conjunction with myself a Volume of such ⟨Poems⟩ stories—and
I inclose you the Title Page of a little forgotten Volume[3] published
by me after Keats's Death—together with the Preface, in which I
refer to the subject.

Private

Will you take the trouble to look at the accompanying
Paraphrase.[4] It will not take much time. My intention has been,
& is, to complete the 4—and publish them, if good enough and
if any Bookseller would be my go-between with the Public. I do
not think Mr Moxon would be likely to deal with my nettles,—

⟨when⟩ since he is accustomed so to be the Florist in his Trade. I must apologize to you for troubling you thus—but you will forgive me.

1. See letter 56, note 3, below, for the history of the canceled preface.
2. Milnes's mother had died on May 1.
3. *The Garden of Florence and Other Poems* (1821).
4. Probably of Juvenal, which he later sent to the publisher Richard Bentley. See his letter to Bentley of 11 March 1848, p. 64.

54

TO RICHARD BENTLEY

11 March 1848

ALS: In the University of Illinois Library.

12 North Crescent
Bedford Square
11 March 1848

Dear Sir

If you are not afraid of publishing satire in the form of 4 paraphrases of Juvenal—adapted to the present day—I will send you one for your perusal—and you shall tell me what you will do with me.

I am in Town for a few days (being now located at the Isle of Wight)[1]—but you will soon be able to judge of the 700 lines— I sample you with—that is supposing you are not averse to a publication of the *kind*.[2]

Have you room for a paper of 7 or 8 pages in the Misc^y.—& if so—when should you have them?

There is something like 3 or 4 Guineas due to me for "The Two Enthusiasts"—published by you about a year ago[3]—will you send them to me per cheque.

Yours very truly
J. H Reynolds

R. Bentley Esq

1. Late in 1847 he had secured an appointment as assistant clerk of the county court at Newport in the Isle of Wight.
2. Bentley rejected it. See the next letter to him.
3. *Bentley's Miscellany*, XXI (February 1847), 209.

55

17 April 1848

Reprinted from *KC*, II, 230–32. Printed by Marsh, *J. H. R.: Poetry and Prose*, pp. 41–42.

Garrick Club
17 Ap^l 1848

My Dear Mr Milnes

Your letter I have had forwarded to me here. I do not in the least understand the mysterious letters you wish information upon. ⟨To⟩ How did you obtain Copies of them?—The source from whence they came *might* give me a clue.

My poor works have been contributions to the London Magazine when Taylor & Hessey had it—a poem published under the title of "Safie" when a Boy—(a downright imitation of Lord Byron, & who refers to it kindly in his printed Journal & letters)[1] —an *Anticipated Parody* of Wordsworth's Peter Bell—also curiously referred to by Ld B. in a printed letter to Moore,[2] written at Venise—in which his Lordship attributes it to Moore himself! a share with Hood[3] in a work called "Odes & addresses to Great Men" of which I should like you to see a Copy—a little work called "The Fancy—being the Memoir & poetical works of Peter Corcoran"—and a small Volume of Poems intitled "The Garden of Florence" by John Hamilton. "—Two of the Poems in the little Book are from Boccacio—& were to have been published with one or two more,—& Keats was to have joined me— but *he* only wrote Isabella & the Pot of Basil."—His illness & death put an end to the work—and I referred to the circumstance in my preface. Forgive so much about that poor obscure—baffled Thing,—myself! I am My Dear Sir

Faithf^y yours
J. H Reynolds

R. M. Milnes Esq

My messenger will wait—but I fear I can be of little use to you. Can I help you on[4] proofs?—but I suppose you are only off for a day or two[5]

1. On 20 February 1814, Byron wrote: "Answered—or rather acknowledged —the receipt of young Reynolds's poem, *Safie*. The lad is clever, but much of his

thoughts are borrowed,—*whence*, the Reviewers may find out. I hate discouraging a young one; and I think,—though wild and more oriental than he would be, had he seen the scenes where he has placed his tale,—that he has much talent, and, certainly fire enough." (Prothero, *Works of Byron*, II, 388; Thomas Moore, *Letters and Journals of Lord Byron*, 3rd ed., 3 vols. [London, 1833], II, 6.) For his letter of thanks to Reynolds see Prothero, *Works of Byron*, III, 45–48.

2. Byron asked Moore on 31 August 1820: "Did you write the lively quiz on Peter Bell? It has wit enough to be yours, and almost too much to be any body else's now going." (Prothero, *Works of Byron*, V, 71; Moore, *Letters and Journals of Byron*, III, 19.)

3. The poet, Reynolds's brother-in-law.

4. Marsh reads, *perhaps correctly*, "as."

5. This postscript is written at the top of the first page.

56

TO RICHARD M. MILNES

22 June 1848

Reprinted from *KC*, II, 234–35. Printed by Marsh, *J. H. R.: Poetry and Prose*, pp. 42–43. The year is not given in the letter, but the comments on the Preface show that this letter was written after that to Milnes of 2 July 1847.

Newport
I of W.
22 June

My Dear Sir

I send you, at this late hour (but I *fear* they will be *in time*!) the 3 Sonnets.[1]

I inclose you a letter of remonstrance, (which I found 28 years old! amongst the originals of Keats's Letters) against the printing the marvellous fragment of Hyperion with a work of Leigh Hunt.[2] I longed to get him free from being a Political adherent to a good, though then dangerous Side for a young Poet.

The Preface is lost.[3]

Do let me hear that the Life is approaching Print-life. I wonder whether the Edingburgh (from which I have been a Stranger for years!)[4] or the Quarterly would permit me to carefully—fairly and *cleanly* ⟨to⟩ review this Life & the works of a true, youthful,—persecuted Poet!

I am Dear Sir
Yours faithf[y]
J. H Reynolds

R. M. Milnes Esq

1. Possibly the Hunt-Shelley-Keats sonnets on the Nile (see *KC*, II, 182, 354–55) or the three sonnets to Keats in Hunt's *Foliage* (1818), for which see Milnes, *Life, Letters, and Literary Remains, of John Keats*, I, 99–101, 148–49.

2. A detail unmentioned by Colvin in *John Keats*, Lowell in *John Keats*, and Dorothy Hewlett in *Adonais: A Life of John Keats* (London: Hurst and Blackett, 1937).

3. Milnes printed it in his 1867 edition, pp. 101–3, from the original manuscript then owned by Moxon and Company. It is now in the Morgan Library, whence H. W. Garrod reprinted it in *The Poetical Works of John Keats* (Oxford: Clarendon Press, 1939), pp. lxxxviii–lxxxix.

4. Keats wrote in December 1818 (*Letters*, II, 7) that Reynolds "has become an edinburgh Reviewer."

57

TO RICHARD BENTLEY

20 July 1848

ALS: In the University of Illinois Library.

Hampshire County Court Office,
Newport, Isle of Wight. [*Letterhead*]
20 July 1848

Dear Sir

Poetry—(or Verses—) make a profitless Book;—are you disposed to treat with me about a *Useful* Book.

I have been arranging for a New Edition (applicable to the present time) the *Birmingham Hutton's* Work on the *Court of Requests*[1]—with a brief memoir and an Introduction bringing the Measure down to its efficacy, at the present Time. I have some valuable notes, from the old Law Authorities, bearing out ⟨this to⟩ the principles of the Measure;—and I shall have the pleasure of dedicating (by his consent) the Book to Sir John Romilly—the Sol. Gen¹.[2]

The Book must be ⟨at⟩ a 6/ or 7/ Book; unless, on consideration, we thought a cheap work better. I think (as I should print the New Act *perhaps*,—) that a moderate price would be the most remunerative![3]

I am Dear Sir
Yours truly
J. H Reynolds

R. Bentley Esq

1. William Hutton (1723–1815), *Court of Requests; their nature, utility, and powers described, with a variety of Cases determined in that of Birmingham* (Birmingham, 1787).

2. John Romilly, first Baron Romilly (1802–74), had been appointed solicitor general in 1848.

3. Reynolds did not know that someone had anticipated him by publishing a revised edition of *Court of Requests* with a memoir in Edinburgh in 1840. Probably Bentley discovered that the need had been met and rejected Reynolds's offer. In any event, Reynolds's version was not published.

58

TO RICHARD M. MILNES

10 August 1848

Reprinted from *KC*, II, 238–40.

Newport
Isle of Wight
10 Augt 1848

My Dear Sir

Valuing Keats's Genius and friendship as I did when he lived;—and loving his memory as I do, now that he is lost to me;— I know not how to express my feelings towards you for the earnestness of your Biography—for your high appreciation of his powers;—for your tender unfolding of his character;—and (*indeed* your only knowing him through his great mind seems to me to enrich all that you write of him!) for the boldness and *clean-ness* of your defence of him against the drunken brawls of Black-wood, and the wicked savagery of Gifford.[1] I love the 2 Volumes![2] I do not seem (to myself) to have known half the cheerfulness— half the vigour,—half the goodness of the heart & mind of Keats, until I met all his letters & Journals ⟨met⟩ *homed* together, and harmonized as they are now, under your care!—I am grateful that he is getting right out into the sunlight!—

—Not however to appear a Rhapsodist in your eyes,—let me thank you from my heart for *all you have done!* I have a copy of the work in sheets—which I shall have interleaved, & in which I shall correct little errors of the press—put queries as to a statem^t here & there—jot down suggestions—note circumstances rising out of your Book on to my recollection, &c &c. A second Edition *must* come;—but I think after I have seen you,—I might help you to a little point of interest here & there, which might be of service.

When do you leave Town?—or rather do you at all return to Town, after a change from the "Speaker at Prayers!" in Westminster,—to the "Heart at its breathings" in the country?— Ever my Dear Sir

Your faithful Friend
J. H Reynolds

R. M. Milnes Esq

Who will review the Book in the Edinburgh;—I wish *almost*, that the task were mine!—Perhaps I should have too much feeling in the case to be a Critic:—And yet I should know the goodness and value of the task committed to my judgment & care!—

1. To whom Reynolds misattributed the attack on *Endymion* in the *Quarterly Review*.

2. Harvard owns the copy inscribed "J. H. Reynolds, with the editor's thanks & regards." Disappointingly enough, it contains almost no comments, none of any importance.

Appendix

1

August(?) 1821

Holograph: In the Beinecke Library at Yale. Though it is undated, the date can be inferred rather closely, since it was intended as a prepublication notice of John Clare's *The Village Minstrel*, published in September 1821.

Town Talk[1]

The Readers of true and natural poetry will hear with much pleasure that a new work from the pen of Clare the Northampton-shire Peasant is on the eve of Publication;—and indeed We feel more than ordinary delight in being enabled to communicate this information, as we believe that ⟨our voice⟩ our pages ⟨are was⟩ were amongst the first to point out the simple beauties of the former volume and the powerful genius of its Author.[2] We have had a sight of the forthcoming work, and it seems to us to evince a very considerable improvement in the language ⟨and rhythm⟩ in which the Author's original and beautiful thoughts are conveyed. It is indeed interesting to observe in many of Clare's new Poems how happily and naturally his refined feelings acquire a refined mode of expression. We have been allowed to extract two poems from the collection,—"The address to the Rural Muse" and a little Ballad entitled "The Request"; the first is singularly sweet and unaffected, and the last possesses in itself that music which makes it a Song at all times whether it be read or sung.

The Rural Muse
(*see printed copy & take it here*)
The Request
(*see printed copy & take it in here*)

The work ⟨is will⟩ forms two handsomely printed volumes and contains a portrait of the Poet and of the Cottage at Helpstone in which he was born and brought up. ⟨We shall take up these Poems and speak of them more⟩

71

1. A search of thirteen likely magazines and newspapers has revealed none with a regular "Town Talk" department. Reynolds almost certainly intended this rejected notice for the *London Magazine*, for which he served as assistant editor and to which he was contributing heavily. Earlier John Scott had included a department called "Town Conversation"; after his death it had lapsed, but late in 1821 John Taylor was thinking of reviving it (Olive Taylor, "John Taylor, Author and Publisher," *London Mercury*, XII [July 1925], 263).

2. The first notice of Clare was Octavius Gilchrist's article in the first number of the *London*, I (January 1820).

2

ALLAN CUNNINGHAM TO REYNOLDS

3 July 1823

ALS: In the Beinecke Library at Yale.

Dear Reynolds

I enclose you a Watt a Wilkie a Rennie a St. Vincent and a Rogers.[1] I have Campbell and Wordsworth and Hogg and Crabbe at your service, let me know if you wish for one

Yours very faithfully
Allan Cunningham

Eccleston S^t. 3 July 1823
To, J. H. Reynolds Esq

1. Cunningham (1784–1842), whom Reynolds knew well as a fellow contributor to the *London Magazine*, served as secretary to the sculptor Francis Chantrey (1781–1840). This note probably accompanied a package containing busts done by Chantrey of the eminent men named: James Watt (1736–1819), the inventor; Sir David Wilkie (1785–1841), painter; John Rennie (1761–1821), designer of Waterloo Bridge; Earl of St. Vincent (1761–1821), naval hero; and Samuel Rogers (1763–1855), poet.

3

FRANCIS FLADGATE TO JAMES WINSTON

5 April 1834

ALS: In the Garrick Club Papers in the Theater Collection at Harvard. James Winston (1779–1843) was secretary to the Garrick Club from its inception in 1831 until his death. Francis Fladgate, Jr., a relative of James Rice, had been a friend of both Reynolds and Keats (*Letters*, I, 181n., 201, 324).

Address: James Winston Esq.

Dear Sir,

M^r. Reynolds gave me the enclosed for you, and explained that absence from Town prevented him sending it sooner.

Yours very faithfully
Francis Fladgate

Brompton
5 April 1834[1]
James Winston Esq

1. The 3 was written hastily to resemble a 7. On the back flap, Fladgate wrote "Mr J H Reynolds."

4

JAMES WINSTON TO REYNOLDS

11 January 1837

This draft letter, which Winston copied and sent, is in the Garrick Club Papers in the Theater Collection at Harvard. Though undated, it must have been written on the 11th, after Reynolds's verse "Farewell to Charles Kemble" was delivered on January 10 and before Reynolds replied on January 12. On the reverse side, someone wrote the names of various members, probably an attendance record at a committee meeting.

Sir

I am directed by the ⟨Garrick Club⟩ Committee to convey to you their most sincere thanks for the very beautiful and affecting lines which produced ⟨such an effect⟩ so great ⟨an⟩ a sensation on ⟨this⟩ tuesday evening.

I have the honor to be

J. H Reynolds Esq

Index

INDEX

Christie, Jonathan H. (*cont.*)
26–28 n, 32–33 n; indicted by coroner's jury, 23; Scott had thought in danger, 30
Christ's Hospital, ix, x, xiii, xxi
Clare, John, xxxiv; contributor to the *London*, xxx; Reynolds notices, 71–72; Reynolds recalls in *London* period, 44. Works: "Address to the Rural Muse," 71; "The Request," 71; *Village Minstrel*, 71
Clarke, Charles Cowden, xxi, xxix
Clifton, xvii
Cockneys, xxiv
Cockney school of English poetry, ix
Colburn, Henry, 50
Coleridge, Samuel T., xxxi
Collier, John P., 39
Colnaghi, Dominic P., 24, 28 n
Comic Annual, 49
Constable, Archibald, xxiii
Corcoran, Peter, xii–xiii, 65
Cosia, T. De Trueba, 40
Cox, Jane, xxii
Cox, William Beckford, x
Crabbe, George, 72
Cripps, Charles, xxvi
Croker, John Wilson, 14
Cunningham, Allan, 44, 72
Curwood, Mr., 30

Dance, George, 45
Darling, Dr. George: confers with Taylor and Reynolds about "Recollections of Keats," 58; his damaging evidence against Patmore, 23, 26–27 n, 29–30, 32–33 n; his evidence annulled, 29; his evidence unlikely to be admitted, 31; his prognosis of Scott's recovery, 30; Reynolds interviews, 29–30; Reynolds recalls in *London* period, 44
D Aurmont, Mme, 53
De Quincey, Thomas, xxx
Devonshire, 3, 14, 35
Dewint, Peter, 21, 22–23
Dickens, Charles, 49
Dilke, Charles W., xxx; cuts price of the *Athenaeum*, xxxi, 37–38; insistence on impartial reviewing, 39; letters to, 37, 37–38, 39, 45;

meets Keats, xxii, 60; Reynolds's contributions to the *London*, xxix. Work: *Papers of a Critic*, xxxiii
Dilke, Maria, xxii, xxxi, 50
Dillon, A. E. A., 40
Dovaston, John, xiv
Dovaston, John F. M., xiv, x. Works: *Fitz-Gwarine with Other Rhymes*, xiv; "Lines to Mrs. Reynolds of Lambeth with a Goose," x, xiv
Drewe, Anne, 10
Drewe, Eliza Powell. *See* Reynolds, Eliza Powell Drewe
Drewe, George, xx n, 9
Drewe, W., 4
Drury Lane, xxviii
Duncan, James, 40
Dunscombe Cliffs, xviii
Duruset, B., 39

Edinburgh Magazine, xxiii, 16
Edinburgh Review, ix, xxiii, 66, 68
Elder, Mr., 30, 32 n
Elgin Marbles, 2
Elliot, Dr. William, 54
Encyclopaedia Brittanica, 39
Examiner, xxiii, xxviii
Exmouth, 22–23

Finch, Anne, Countess of Winchelsea, 1–2
Fladgate, Francis, Jr., 72–73
Fladgate, Francis, Sr., xxiii
Follett, Mr., 54
Forman, Maurice B., xxxiii, xxxv

Garrick Club, 45, 48, 73; petition for a smoking room, 48; Reynolds's membership in, xxxi, 38; letters to, 39–40, 61–62; Reynolds acknowledges thanks of, 41–42
Gentleman's Magazine, xiv, xvi, xxxiii, 1–2
Gifford, William, 68
Gittings, Robert, xx n, xxiv
Gleig, Hamilton, xxvi
Green, H. G., xxvii, xxx
Griffin, John, xiii
Guthrie, Dr. George J., 30, 32 n

Hackney, x
Hamilton family, x

INDEX

Keats, John (*cont.*)
toward Hunt, xxviii–xxix; birth
date, 60, 62–63; changes publishers,
xxii; Charlotte Cox Reynolds in his
letters, x; collaboration with Reynolds on imitations of Boccaccio,
65; compared with Shakespeare,
59; copy of Reynolds's sonnet sent
to, 7; departure for Italy, 21; disap-
proves treatment of Jane Cox, xxii;
Garden of Florence compared with
Lamia volume, xxv; judgment of
Bailey's treatment of Mariane Reynolds, xxvii; judgment of Reynolds
in Haydon quarrel, xxvi; letters to,
12–13, 15; letters to Reynolds, 56,
57; meets Reynolds's friends, xxii;
personality attracts Reynolds, xxi;
politics, 19, 66; reaction to Reynolds's report of meeting with
Hunt, xxviii; Reynolds and Blackwood, xxiv; Reynolds introduces to
family, xxi–xxii; Reynolds met, 60;
Reynolds not forgetful of, 14–15;
Reynolds pained by Hessey's account of, 18; Reynolds requests
proof of *Endymion*, 12; Reynolds
reviews *Endymion*, xxii; Reynolds
reviews *Poems* of 1817, xxii; Reynolds's account of, to Jeffrey, 19;
Reynolds's services to, xxii; Reynolds's subordination of himself
to, xxiii; Reynolds welcomes into
circle, xxi; Severn's letter on his
death, 36; stimulated Reynolds's
writing, xxiii. Works: *Endymion*,
xxii, xxviii, 61, 63; *Endymion*, first
preface to, 61, 62, 66; the great
odes, xxv; *Hyperion*, xxv, xxviii–
xxix; *Isabella*, xxii, xxv, 12–13,
63, 65; *Lamia* volume, xxv, 18;
"Ode to a Nightingale," 63; "Ode
to Psyche," 63; "On the Sea,"
5; *Poems* of 1817, xxii; "Robin
Hood," xxii; "Think Not of It,
Sweet One," 63; *To J. H. Reynolds,
Esq.*, xii
Keats, Thomas, xxxi, xxxiv
Keats-Shelley Journal, xxxiii
Kelley, Frances, xxxi
Kemble, Charles, 41–42, 73
King's Theatre, 42

Lamb, Charles, xiii, xvi, xxx, xxxi,
44
Lambeth, xv, xx, xxi
Lambeth Boys Parochial School, ix
Lambeth Female Asylum, ix, xxi, 17
Langley, Henry, xvi
Laporte, P. F.: letters to, 42, 43
Law, 60, 67
Leigh, Mary, xvii–xx; letters to, 7-10,
10–11
Leigh, Mrs., 11
Leigh, Sarah, xvii–xx, xix–xx, 10, 11
Leigh, Thomasine, xvii–xx, xxvii, 10,
11
Leigh-Browne-Lockyer   Collection,
xviii
Leigh sisters, xxvi, xxviii
Lin Tse-su, xxxiv, 50
"Lion's Head," 31
Literary Gazette, 18
Little Britain, xxi–xxii, xxx
Lockhart, John G., xxiv, 25, 26 n
London, x, xiii
London Magazine, xxxi, 65; duel, 26 n,
28 n; first to notice John Clare,
71; poems in about Reynolds's
schooling, xi; Reynolds procras-
tinates drama for, 36; Reynolds
recommended as contributor, 16 n;
Reynolds's contributions to, xxix–
xxx; Reynolds sends circulars to
contributors to, 25; Reynolds soli-
cited to contribute, 16; Reynolds's
recollection of its great days, 44;
Taylor owns rights to articles in,
43
London Morning Chronicle, 24, 40–41
Longman's, 43
Longmore, Eliza Beckford Reynolds,
x, xi, xxx
Louisa Venoni, xix
Lumley, Benjamin, 42

McCullock, John R., xxxiv, 25
Mackenzie, Robert S.: letter to, 55
Macready, William, 40
Marsh, George L., xxxiii
Martin, John, xvi, xvii, xxii, xxvi
Martin, Miss (John's sister), xvii,
xxvi
Masefield, John, xii
Matthews, Charles, xxxi

INDEX

Reynolds, John Hamilton (*cont.*)
Patmore, xxix; collaboration with Keats on imitations of Boccaccio, 65; connection with the *Athenaeum*, xxxi–xxxii; contributes to the *Champion*, xvii; contributes to the *Inquirer*, xvi; contributes to the *Gentleman's Magazine*, xvi; contributes to the *London*, xxix–xxx; death of first love, xvi; desire for fame at Shrewsbury School, xii–xiii; difficulty in editing the *New Sporting Magazine*, 49; dismissed as Hood's attorney, xxxii; Dovaston's sonnet to, xiv; enters law, xxiii; escapes Hood's quarrel with his family, xxxii; flattered by Lockhart, xxiv; forbids Moxon to publish Keats's letter to him, 57; friendship with Haydon, xxi; heavy drinking in last years, xvi, xxxii; his abundant writing during friendship with Keats, xxiii; his bankruptcy, xxxii, 49; his birth, xi; his gratitude to Milnes, 68; his illness, xxiii, 11–12, 50, 54, 62; his interleaved copy of Milnes's *Life of Keats*, 68; his services to Keats, xxii; his skeleton of a reputation, 43; intends to write his recollections of Keats, 57–58; introduces Keats to his friends, xxii; junior clerkship at the Amicable Assurance Society, xiii; leaves Amicable Assurance Society, xx; list of his works, 65; marriage, xxx; meets Bailey, xviii; meets Byron, xvi; meets Eliza Drewe, xx; meets the Leighs, xx; meets Rice, xviii; met Keats, 60; moves to Little Britain, xxi–xxii; moves to Isle of Wight, xxxii; moves to 19 Lamb's Conduit St., xxi; name from mother's relatives, x; persuaded Keats to replace first preface to *Endymion*, 61; plan to publish with Keats, 13, 63; plans to collect articles for a book, 43–44; procrastinates drama for the *London*, 36; promises to aid Milnes, 59; quarrel with Haydon, xxv–xxvi; reconciliation with Bailey, xxvii; rejects Blackwood's offer, xxiv; relations with Hunt, xxvii–xxix; renunciation of poetry, 13; resolves on marriage, xxiii; sends Hunt a copy of *The Naiad*, xxi; sends Wordsworth a copy of *The Naiad*, xx; serves as Poet Ferneat, xv–xvi; subordinates himself to Keats, xxiii; theatrical writing, xxxi; urges Keats to publish, 15; vacillation between law and literature, xxiii; visits Drewes in Exeter, xx; welcomes Keats into circle, xxi; wishes to review Milnes's *Life of Keats*, 66; with Rice plans opera, xix; writes tragedy, xix; writes verse at Shrewsbury School, xii–xiii; writes verse for the *Athenaeum*, 39. Works: *Confounded Foreigners*, xxxi, 45; *The Eden of Imagination*, xiv, xvi, xxvii; "The Experiences of the Bivouacs" (rejected), 53; *The Fancy*, xii–xiii, xxiii, xxiv, 65; "Farewell to the Muses," xxiii; *The Garden of Florence and Other Poems*, xxiii, xxiv, xxv, 63, 65; *Gil Blas*, xxxi; *The Ladye of Provence*, xxv; "Living Authors: A Dream," xxix; *The Naiad*, xx, xxii, 3, 5; *A New Entertainment*, xxxi; *Odes and Addresses to Great People*, xvi, xxxi, 65; *An Ode* (on the overthrow of Napoleon), xvii; "Ode to Friendship," xiv; "Old Ballads," xi–xii; *One, Two, Three, Four, Five: By Advertisement*, xxiv; "On Fighting," xxix, 16; paper on the Winds (rejected), 47; "A Parthian Peep at Life," xi; *Peter Bell*, xxiv, 65; "Pilgrimage of the Living Poets," xxiii, xxviii, xxix; *Recollections* (of Fanny Kelley), xxxi; "Reflections of Mirth," xv–xvi; *The Romance of Youth*, xxv; *Safie*, xvi, 65–66; "Some Passages in the Lives of Wooden Legs," 47; "Sonnet to Haydon," 7; "Stanzas to the Memory of Richard Allen," xi; "Think of Me," 55; "Town Talk," 71–72; "Turfiana," 46; "The Two Enthusiasts," 64; "Varieties," 46

Reynolds, Lucy, xxxii

Reynolds, Mariane, xi, xxii, xxvii, xxx

80

INDEX

Thackeray, William M., xxxi, 47
Times (London), xxxiii, 13–14, 24, 32 n
Titian, 9
Tottenham, x
Traill, James, 23, 24, 26–28 n, 32–33 n

Vale of Health, 60
Victoria, Queen, 50

Waldegrave, William, Baron Radstock, 17
Ward, Ned, Jr. (Reynolds's pseudonym), xi
Watt, James, 72
Wedlake, W. B., xiii
Westminster Review, xxxi
Westmoreland, 49
White, W. F., 40
Wilkie, Sir David, 72
Wilson, John, xxxi
Winchelsea. *See* Finch, Anne, Countess of Winchelsea

Winston, James: his letter to Reynolds, 73; letters to, 38, 41–42, 44–45, 48
Woodhouse, Richard, xxxi, 21, 23; accompanied Keats to Gravesend, 22; copied Keats's letters to Reynolds without permission, 57; his MS book of Keats's letters and poems, 58–59; his unselfish attitude toward Keats, 59; meets Keats, xxii
Wordsworth, William, 72; copy of *The Naiad* sent to, xx, 5; praise of, 5; Reynolds's parody of *Peter Bell*, 65; Reynolds's letter to, 2. Works: *An Evening Walk*, xvi; *Peter Bell*, xxiv; "Poems on the Naming of Places," xviii; "Resolution and Independence," 12
Worsley, Henry, 13–14

Yates, Thomas, xiv
Yellow Dwarf, xxiii, xxvi, xxviii, xxxiii

Zilia (Thomasine Leigh), xvii